RCML

STRANGE WORLD

A modern myth, or evidence of life on other planets? Sightings of
U.F.O.s ('Unidentified Flying Objects') are reported worldwide.

Britain's best-known ancient monument, Stonehenge was begun in c.1900 B.C., to calculate and celebrate astronomical events. In modern times it has housed seasonal festivals of 'alternative' movements from 'Druids' to Morris dancers, until these were banned in 1985 to protect the site.

MYSTERIOUS FACTS
STRANGE WORLD

RICHARD O'NEILL

Grange
BOOKS

CLB 3029

© 1993 Colour Library Books Ltd., Godalming, Surrey, England.

Published by Grange Books
An Imprint of Grange Books Limited
The Grange
Grange Yard
London
SE1 3AG

Published 1993

ISBN 1 85627 399 7

Printed and bound in Italy

The Author
Richard O'Neill was born in Northampton, England. He has been a soldier, professional boxer, labourer, actor, and writer of fiction, comic strips, and stage and television plays. In recent years he has specialized in historical non-fiction. His book *Suicide Squads: Special Attack Weapons of World War II* was published in Britain and the U.S.A. in 1981, and in Japan in 1988. He is co-author of two books on toy collecting, and has edited and contributed to many books on military history and weaponry. He was a major contributor to *Lands and Peoples*, a multi-volume work published in the U.S.A. and other countries in 1990-92. His books on *World War II* and *The Middle Ages* recently appeared in the U.S.A., and his *Men and Monsters* is a companion volume in the 'Mysterious Facts' series.

Credits
Editor: Philip de Ste. Croix
Designer: Jill Coote
Picture research: Leora Kahn
Production: Ruth Arthur, Sally Connolly, Neil Randles
Director of Production: Gerald Hughes
Typesetting: SX Composing Ltd.
Colour separations: Scantrans Pte Ltd., Singapore
Printed and bound by New Interlitho SpA, Italy

For many years scholars did not believe the enigmatic giant statues of Easter Island in the Pacific were the work of the islanders, but ascribed them to visitors from other cultures – or even outer space.

CONTENTS

Searchlight on U.F.O.s

Like its companion titles *Men and Monsters* and *Gods and Demons*, this book celebrates the mysterious, odd, bizarre and, sometimes, macabre. The greater part of this volume deals with the natural (or unnatural) wonders of Earth. I have scanned the planet's skies and oceans for 'space ships'; wondered whether it is really flat – or hollow; considered some of its meteorological and biological marvels, from 'Northern Lights' to talking beasts; and pried into the secrets of its strangest places. Finally, I have examined, and sometimes questioned, some of the strange beliefs and even stranger behaviour of its peoples.

The COMING of the SAUCERS

By Kenneth Arnold & Ray Palmer

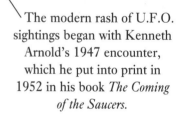

The modern rash of U.F.O. sightings began with Kenneth Arnold's 1947 encounter, which he put into print in 1952 in his book *The Coming of the Saucers*.

In 1967 a Colorado weather station technician took an ordinary landscape photo – and discovered this 'flying saucer' image only when the picture was developed.

Unlike former President Jimmy Carter, I have never seen an Unidentified Flying Object (U.F.O.) and I am by no means convinced of the existence of the alien craft described in the first part of this book. But it seems that if the U.S. electorate voted the straight U.F.O. ticket, Carter would have remained in office in perpetuity. In 1991 a Gallup poll revealed that some 50 per cent of Americans believe there is some form of extra-terrestrial life. Fair enough, so do many scientists – in 1992 N.A.S.A.'s radio telescopes began a ten-year scan through the Milky Way galaxy for extra-terrestrial intelligences (E.T.I.s) – and so do I, although I do not expect to find a message from 'E.T.' on my answerphone. But the same poll revealed that 47 per cent of Americans believe U.F.O.s are real –

Kenneth Arnold – whose sighting of nine 'flying saucers' on June 24, 1947, began the U.F.O. mania – to Timothy Good's bestselling *Alien Liaison* (1991), which has an approving commentary by Admiral of the Fleet, Lord Hill-Norton, Britain's former Chief of Defence Staff. Some were out to lunch: others, like Good's work, sober and well argued. But one thing that bothered me was how speculations and rumours printed by Ufologists in the 1950s-60s somehow became 'established facts' in the books of some of their successors in the 1970s-80s. Nor do I like the argument that if a government department or other official body has 'no comment' on a supposed marvel, then there must be something in it – and if it issues a flat denial, then what is denied must be true, or why should they bother to deny it?

A sense of wonder is a fine thing. But then so is commonsense.

Today scientists explain away eerie 'Northern Lights' as a matter of electrically charged solar particles; in earlier times they seemed as unearthly as any U.F.O.

This photograph purports to show an alien corpse in the wreckage of a 'flying saucer' which crashed in New Mexico in 1948 – but many find it unconvincing.

and 14 per cent claim to have seen one.

My reluctance to go all the way with U.F.O. believers may some day put me in the company of those who advised the Wright Brothers to stick with repairing bicycles, along with former British Astronomer Royal Sir Richard Woolley, who in 1956 announced: 'Space travel is utter bilge.' And if you believe in U.F.O.s – or the Hollow Earth, or King Tut's curse, or any other of the beliefs examined in this book – then I respect your right to do so and I am prepared to listen to your arguments. Provided they are convincing ones.

Researching U.F.O.s, I consulted sources ranging from *The Coming of the Saucers* (1952) by

Natural wonders

In 1992 Dr. Ari Ben-Menahem of Israel's Weizmann Institute of Science theorized that some 'miraculous' happenings detailed in the *Old Testament* could be attributed to natural phenomena. The destruction of Sodom and Gomorrah, he believes, may have been caused by a well authenticated earthquake in c.1560 B.C. King David's vision of 'the Angel of the Lord with a sword in his hand' (*First Chronicles*: Chapter 21; Verse 16) may refer to the appearance in 986 B.C. of what we now know as Halley's Comet. The *Book of Joshua* (Chapter 10; Verse 13) tells how Joshua successfully commanded the Sun to stand still over Gibeon, so daylight lasted until the Amorites were defeated. A few verses earlier we are told that 'the Lord cast down great stones from Heaven'. Dr. Ben-Menahem thinks this may refer to a meteor shower, pointing out that reports of the Tunguska meteor of 1908 say that after its explosion night

The 'Andes Candelabrum' drawn in the desert of Paracas, Peru. Why, and how, did ancient peoples create such giant 'landscape drawings' visible only to the gods – and to modern aircraft?

Today we know who carved the Easter Island statues, and how – but whether they represent gods or chieftains remains a mystery.

was turned into bright daylight for several hours.

The Tunguska meteor is one of several 'natural wonders' examined in the second part of this book. Some are spectacular, like the comets which our ancestors looked on as signs and omens. Some are still unexplained, like the footprints of humans in ancient rocks where, according to science, no human could have trod. Some, like strange rains of frogs and other creatures, and 'crop circles', may have a simple explanation.

There follows a tour of some of Earth's most mysterious places. They range from the very real and impressive remains of northern and southern Native American civilizations to more controversial locations like the Bermuda Triangle and other 'hoodoo seas', and fabled Atlantis and other 'lost continents'. I think it is a pity that so many able and interesting writers have chosen to concentrate on the latter, when so many real places of mystery remain underexplored. To my mind the origin of such things as Britain's 'chalk giants' (examined here) is of more interest than speculation as to whether the inhabitants of Shangri-La knew the secret of negative gravity. And let us solve the real mysteries surrounding the Easter Island heads (also examined here) before we begin conjecturing whether they were erected by supermen or 'alien gods' from outer space.

This section ends with a look at curses, jinxes and hexes. It seems to me that although certain famous 'curses' have gained weight with each retelling (I hope my examination of the curse of Tutankhamun's tomb does not further varnish the tale), it cannot be denied that even mundane artifacts like warships, automobiles and locomotives seem sometimes to act as a focus for ill luck. The chain of unpleasant circumstances that binds them cannot be wholly ascribed to what has been named 'synchronicity', a succession of seemingly meaningful coincidences. A personal curse is rather different: rather than attribute its working to some supernatural power wielded by the curser, I am inclined to believe that it will work just so far as the victim believes it will.

A modern puzzle: are the widely reported 'crop circles' in cornfields created by freak weather conditions, visitors from outer space, or hoaxers?

Modern popular tradition associates the treasures of ancient Egypt with sinister tales of cursed tombs and murderous mummies.

13

Improbable: impossible?

The final section of this book is given over to a miscellany of mysteries and oddities, ranging from prophets of doom to raisers of the dead – even eaters of the dead; taking in a selection of unexplained appearances and disappearances, including the alleged 'teleportation' of a World War II destroyer escort; and ending with a look at popular superstitions and 'urban legends'.

These latter – the one about the microwaved cat (always the pet of a 'friend of a friend' of the raconteur) is perhaps the archetype – are truly strange and fascinating. Also, I believe, useful – as

The late ex-King Zog I haunted his Rolls Royce – or so the scent of cigarettes persuaded its new owner. Smells – from mystery fragrance to grave-stench – often suggest ghosts.

many aspects of the mysterious, however intriguing, are not. Some of the urban legends I have collected are really moral fables for our time, illustrating the dangers of drug taking and casual sex.

Readers may think I have been over sceptical about some aspects of 'the unexplained' examined in this book and its companion volumes. I once lost a good friend through such scepticism. He owned for a time an armoured Rolls Royce automobile (he was a dealer in such exotica) that had belonged to Albania's ex-King Zog I (1895-1961). It was, he claimed, haunted: often, the distinctive smell of the monarch's Turkish cigarettes filled its interior. I commented that unless he had had the upholstery renewed this was not surprising: Zog was one of the world's champion smokers, lighting up some 240 per day.

Although I am sceptical when it comes to U.F.O.s, 'space gods', and 'lost continents', I accept that there is much in this world

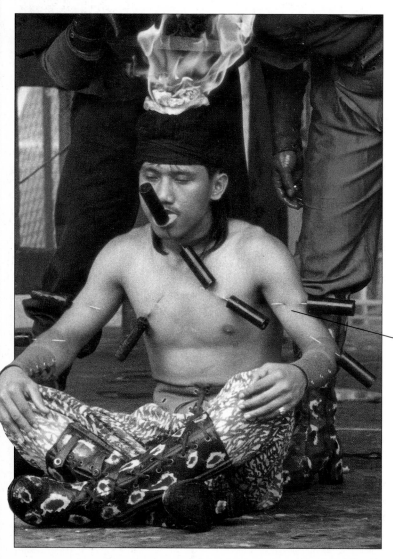

By prayer and fasting the human body can apparently break natural laws: this Muslim ascetic endures weighted daggers through his flesh without pain or even bleeding.

Prehistoric monuments were long thought to have healing powers. Until recent times sick people crawled through the holed stone of the Men-an-tol (Cornwall, England) to seek a cure.

that we do not, and perhaps never shall, understand. In investigating 'mysterious facts' I have borne in mind the advice of the immortal Sherlock Holmes: '. . . when you have eliminated the impossible, whatever remains, however improbable, must be the truth'. (And I have not forgotten that Holmes's creator, Sir Arthur Conan Doyle, whom I admire above most men, was himself a true believer in the supernatural – as readers of other books in this series will know.)

But who is to say what 'the impossible' is? Perhaps the true *guru* of all lovers of the mysterious fact – all those who would like to able to believe, like Lewis Carroll's Duchess, in two or three impossible things before breakfast; and that is most of us, including this writer – is the German physicist Werner Karl Heisenberg (1901-76). In the late 1920s his studies led him to the conclusion that it was impossible to know everything there was

Amulets to ward off evil date back to ancient times and range from natural objects like a holed pebble to this Turkish 'hand of Fatima'.

to know about a sub-atomic particle at any given moment. His formulation of this 'Uncertainty Principle' was bitterly opposed by Einstein, among others, but is now accepted by many scientists, some of whom speak of an 'unseen world' below the threshold of observed reality. Its relevance to the 'strange world' of this book is obvious.

Visitors from space?

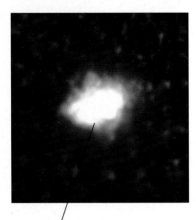

A number of N.A.S.A. astronauts have reported sighting – and, as seen here, have even photographed – 'Unidentified Flying Objects' in space.

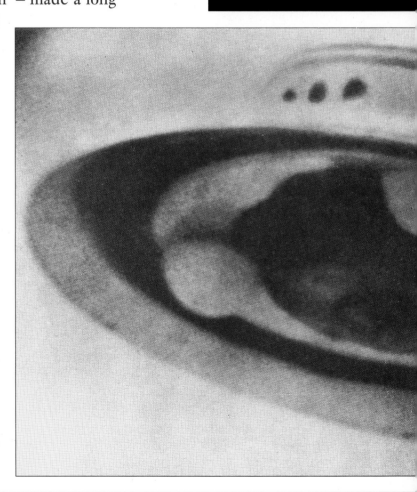

On June 24, 1947, Idaho businessman Kenneth Arnold, flying his private plane near Mount Ranier, Wash., sighted 9 discs, each c.30m (100ft) in diameter, flying in formation at c.2,735kmh (1,700mph). Soon many similar reports were made worldwide – but it was Arnold's description of how they 'skipped like saucers across water' that gave the world's press a name for them: 'flying saucers'. Today we call them 'Unidentified Flying Objects' (U.F.O.s), and those who study them 'Ufologists'. Many believe they are visitors from outer space, crewed by extra-terrestrial beings (E.T.s).

Scientists attributed Arnold's sighting, and many others, to 'unusual atmospheric conditions', but the U.S. Air Force – in Cold War days, perhaps fearing a Soviet 'secret weapon' – made a long study of U.F.O.s. Its 'Project Blue Book' (1950-69) examined some 12,000 sightings, concluding that most were of mundane objects and denying there was any evidence that U.F.O.s were craft from another planet. Recent polls show that nearly 50 per cent of Americans (and similarly large minorities in other countries) disagree. Some Ufologists say they have been with us since the beginning of time: that our ideas of gods are based on E.T.s who sowed the seeds of civilization on Earth. Some say they come from within our 'Hollow Earth' or from beneath our oceans (see later pages). Perhaps they are the craft of benevolent aliens who protect us from some extra-terrestrial threat – or perhaps their crews are carrying out reconnaissance for a coming invasion. Psychiatrist Carl Jung theorized that U.F.O.s filled 'a religious vacuum' for modern humanity, representing 'a hope . . . the expectation of a saviour'. A recent view is that U.F.O.s exist not in reality, but as paranormal phenomena – 'ghosts' for our troubled times.

This photograph was taken through the window of a Parisian building: the Eiffel Tower 'U.F.O.' is the reflection of an electric lamp and shade on the window pane.

The U.S. Air Force released this photograph of a glowing 'disc', brighter than the Moon (on right of picture), but did not say it was a U.F.O.

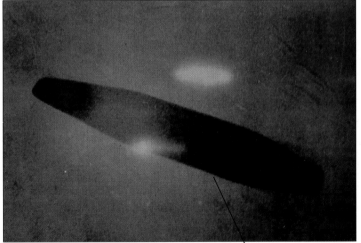

George Adamski's famous photograph, taken at Palomar Gardens, California, in December 1952, is said to show a spacecraft from Venus.

Another of Adamski's Californian photographs: this is claimed to show an 'interplanetary carrier ship' and two 'scout craft'.

FACT FILE

❏ Reports of strange craft in Earth's skies date back some 3,000 years: some exponents of 'the gods were astronauts' theories say that the Old Testament prophet Ezekiel's vision of four 'living creatures' and a 'wheel' (*Ezekiel*: Chapter 1; Verses 4-28) describes an encounter with 'space gods' and their craft. The great Sanskrit epic *Mahabharata*, probably composed c.300 B.C., tells of gods fighting in the sky in aircraft (*vimanas*) with laser-like weapons.

❏ In 1968 a University of Colorado team headed by Dr. Edward U. Condon (above), Professor of Astrophysics, produced a 1,465-page report based on data from the U.S.A.F.'s 'Project Blue Book'. The 'Condon Report', seen as authoritative by 'Ufo-sceptics', said at least 90 per cent of U.F.O. sightings were caused by 'ordinary objects' and that most of the others were of dubious worth, and concluded: 'Nothing has come from the study of U.F.O.s . . . that has added to scientific knowledge.'

The Martians are coming!

Makers of fictions favour 'red planet' Mars as a likely source of alien invasion. This owes much to U.S. astronomer Percival Lowell (1855-1916), whose many real accomplishments (including prediction of the existence of planet Pluto, confirmed in 1930) are shadowed by his 'discovery' of life on Mars. In 1894, after observing 'channels' (Italian: *canali*) there noted by Italian astronomer Giovanni Schiaparelli, Lowell pronounced them 'canals', built by Martians struggling to irrigate their desert planet by chanelling water from its ice-caps. Some believed in the Martians and their canals until photographs taken by 'Mariner' space probes in the 1960s-70s showed they did not exist. Lowell's speculations triggered the U.S. 'airship scare' of 1896-97. Rumour said a large, cigar-shaped propeller-driven dirigible (no dirigible nor aircraft would fly in the U.S.A. until 1903), perhaps from Mars, was making a trans-continental journey from west to east. Letters to prominent Americans were produced, said to have been dropped by the 'Martians': one to the great inventor Edison, who denounced the affair as a hoax. Britain's 'scareships' of 1909-13 were a product of war fears. The night-flying dirigibles, c.70m (230ft) long and very fast, were said to be crewed not by Martians but Germans (whose Zeppelin airships would attack Britain in reality after war came in 1914). War rumours also helped fuel the U.S.A.'s 'Martian scare' of October 30, 1938, when actor Orson Welles's Mercury Theater of the Air broadcast a dramatization of *The War of the Worlds* by H.G. Wells. It was so realistic that many persons believed Martians had landed at Princeton, N.J., and were slaughtering with death rays all who opposed them. Some prepared to flee their homes, while across the nation police and military posts were deluged with alarms and calls for help.

'Red planet' Mars, as seen from a 'Viking' spacecraft. No signs of life were found on the planet at the sites examined by the 'Viking' missions' landers.

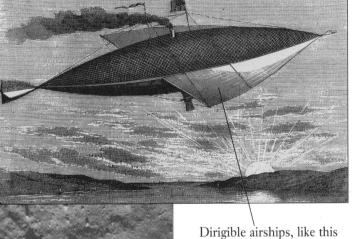

Martian fighting machines ravage Earth – in the movie *The War of the Worlds* (1952). Some radio listeners in 1938 believed they really faced this peril.

Dirigible airships, like this visionary 'steam carriage' of 1863, were a mainstay of science-fiction – and a source of many popular 'scare stories' – until the early 20th century.

Many early sci-fi tales told of 'Moon men': but the first living beings to imprint the ancient dust of the 'Sea of Tranquillity' were the astronauts of the 'Apollo 11' landing in 1969.

❏ Some astronomers suggest Lowell (below) was misled by huge dust storms that periodically sweep the arid surface of Mars. They say the storms occasionally create an effect resembling the 'network of straight lines' seen by Schiaparelli and Lowell.

❏ The 'airship scare' of 1896-97 produced tales as bizarre as any reported by Ufologists. A farmer in Sioux City, Ia., claimed he had been caught by a grappling hook from an airship and dragged some distance before struggling free. A Michigan man claimed a voice 'from above the clouds' had ordered him to fetch 48 egg salad sandwiches and a pot of coffee – and had let down a basket to receive them.

❏ A wave of 'airship sightings' hit Texas in April 1897, when it was said 'Mr. Wilson of Illinois' was chugging around the state in an advanced airship of his own design. Several Texans claimed to have spoken to him when he dropped in on their properties.

Close encounters

Dr. J. Allen Hynek, an astronomer who became convinced of the reality of U.F.O.s while working on 'Project Blue Book', divided sightings into three classes. 'Close encounters of the first kind' are when a U.F.O. is seen aloft or on the ground. In 'second kind' encounters it leaves behind evidence of its presence, such as marks on the ground. 'Third kind' encounters are when alien beings are sighted. These are the most controversial. Most scientists say that if E.T.s exist it is most unlikely they would look like humans, having evolved very differently. Yet c.90 per cent of persons claiming to have met with aliens describe them as humanoid, ranging from tiny 'goblins' to handsome 'supermen'. Sceptics point out that, from George Adamski's famous encounter with a 'Venusian' in 1952 onward, most folk have described encounters in standard sci-fi terms: the aliens wear 'metallic space suits', often carry 'ray guns', and, surprisingly, are fluent in the language of those they meet. Even those who do not conform to such patterns are 'B movie' characters: hulking robots or 'bug eyed monsters'. Some Ufologists add to Hynek's classifications 'close encounters of the fourth kind': when humans are abducted by aliens, who may take them into their craft for examination or experimentation, sometimes using hypnotic or telepathic powers to take over their minds. An added peril of a 'fourth kind' encounter is that the human subject may later be visited by 'Men in Black' (M.I.B.s). These sinister persons (very occasionally women) typically arrive in black Cadillacs (outdated models, but apparently brand new), produce U.S.A.F. or C.I.A. type identity documents (although some say the M.I.B.s themselves are E.T.s), and warn 'fourth kind' encounterers that to speak of their experiences could have unpleasant consequences.

From information given by Betty and Barney Hill during deep trance therapy, an artist produced portraits of the aliens who abducted the New Hampshire couple in 1961.

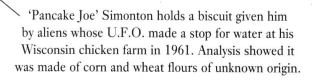

'Pancake Joe' Simonton holds a biscuit given him by aliens whose U.F.O. made a stop for water at his Wisconsin chicken farm in 1961. Analysis showed it was made of corn and wheat flours of unknown origin.

Travis Walton claimed to have been taken up by a U.F.O. (seen also by five of his workmates) in a National Forest near Heber, Ariz., on November 5, 1975. Missing for five days, he reappeared in a telephone booth 24km (15mi) away.

Police patrolman Lonnie Zamora saw an oval U.F.O. some 5m (16ft) long land near Soccoro, N.Mex., in April 1964. Two aliens briefly exited the craft.

Apparently alarmed by Zamora's approach, the aliens re-entered their craft and blasted off. He immediately examined the site, placing stones to outline marks left by the U.F.O.'s 'landing legs'.

❑ A fairly high proportion of 'fourth kind' encounters seem to relate to sexual fantasies: many men and women claim to have had sexual intercourse, either forced or voluntary, with E.T.s. In 1966 a Melbourne, Australia, woman claimed to be pregnant after rape by a 'handsome alien'. Most reports of 'sexual encounters of the fourth kind' seem to originate from South America. Perhaps stories about the superiority of 'Latin lovers' have spread through space.

❑ Very many cases of cattle mutilation (above) throughout the U.S.A. from c.1963 to the present have been blamed on E.T.s 'taking samples'. Mysterious lights in the sky, or unidentified aircraft, have been reported by police patrols and ranchers who have lost stock. Other suspects include Satanic cultists; even the U.S. military or C.I.A., supposedly using the unfortunate beasts in secret weaponry experiments. But after a particularly severe outbreak of mutilations in New Mexico in 1979, a government funded inquiry reported that all were 'consistent with . . . normal predation, scavenger activity, and normal decomposition of a dead animal'.

Mistaken identity?

Many reports of U.F.O. sightings stem from strange 'lights in the sky', like this striking example. Sceptics attribute most to meteorological phenomena.

Although some say the 'aliens among us' have sinister motives, only one person has died as a direct result of alleged U.F.O. activity. On January 7, 1948, when a 'saucer' was reported over Kentucky, Capt. Thomas Mantell, U.S.A.F., pursued in a P-51 Mustang. He radioed from c.6,100m (20,000ft): 'appears metallic . . . tremendous size . . . following up'. His wrecked plane was found later that day. Some claimed it had exploded in midair; there were rumours that no body was found, or that the corpse bore marks of a 'death ray'. The U.S.A.F. believes the 'U.F.O.' was a huge U.S. Navy 'Skyhook' balloon (then semi-secret) used to carry scientific instruments into the upper atmosphere, its aluminiumized fabric catching sunlight to give a 'saucer' effect. At c.9,000m (30,000ft) in an aircraft without oxygen equipment, Mantell lost consciousness and crashed.

Hannah McRoberts was intent on a landscape photograph on Canada's Vancouver Island, October 1981. Neither she nor her husband spotted the U.F.O. until the film was developed.

Sceptics think almost all U.F.O. sightings, and most photographs that are not faked, are cases of mistaken identity. Although very few aircraft are actually saucer shaped (exceptions include experimental models like the U.S. Navy's Chance Vought 'Flying Flapjack' and U.S. Army's Avro-Canada 'Avrocar'), mis-identifications of low flying aircraft are said to account for 17 per cent of all U.F.O.s; aircraft vapour trails that break up into strange shapes are another source. Many 'U.F.O.s' prove to be as ordinary as the reflections of automobile or street lights from low cloud or fog. Natural phenomena like ball lightning and lenticular ('lens shaped') cloud formations account for a few sightings, but experts say that nearly one third of all U.F.O.s prove to be sightings of the planet Venus – exceeded in brightness only by the Sun and Moon – or of comets, meteors or the debris of man-made satellites re-entering Earth's atmosphere.

After computer analysis, U.F.O. experts said Villa's picture was probably faked.

'Lenticular' clouds like this, usually formed by rising air currents in hilly country, may seem convincing 'saucers'. Further, they often appear to move in regular formations.

Paul Villa claimed this shot taken near Albuquerque, N.Mex., in 1963, showed a 'star ship' whose nine-being crew spoke with him for some 90 minutes.

❑ In 1944-45 Allied night fighter pilots over Germany reported trouble with red or silver 'balls of fire', apparently in controlled flight, that flew alongside and buzzed them, sometimes causing instruments to malfunction. Some suggested they were 'alien craft', but official sources, having at first suspected a radio-controlled 'psychological weapon', later attributed the 'Foo Fighters' (below), as the pilots named them, to 'hallucination under combat stress'.

❑ In October 1973 Governor James Earl 'Jimmy' Carter of Georgia, later U.S. president, filed an official report on a U.F.O. he sighted, in company with 20 other persons, in Leary, Ga., on January 6, 1969. Experts believe that the object he viewed ('the darndest thing I've ever seen') – described as being some 30 degrees above the horizon and a little smaller than the Moon – was the planet Venus, but in 1976 President Carter still insisted: 'I am convinced that U.F.O.s exist because I've seen one.'

Is anyone out there?

The 'Apollo 8' mission lifts off on December 21, 1968, on the way to make the first manned circumnavigation of the Moon.

Scientists estimate that the Milky Way galaxy, in which Earth lies, contains c.100,000,000,000 stars, of which 10 per cent may have habitable planets. Some hope that contact with extra-terrestrial intelligences (E.T.I.s) may soon be achieved. The first practical steps were taken by U.S. 'Mariner' space probes which flew by Venus, Mars and Mercury in the 1960s-70s, and by the 'Viking' unmanned landings on Mars in 1976. In 1992 N.A.S.A. announced a $120,000,000, 10-year 'alien hunt'. In an attempt to detect radio signals from 1,000 stars within 100 light years of Earth, the huge Arecibo, Puerto Rico, radio telescope will examine each one for about 17 minutes. The movable Goldstone radio dish in California's Mojave Desert will make unlimited sweeps through the galaxy. Some hold that E.T.I.s have already attempted radio contact with us. Around 1900 radio pioneers Nikola Tesla (1856-1943) and Guglielmo Marconi (1874-1937) claimed to have received recognizable signals from space. It is claimed that 'voices in an unknown language' interrupted astronaut Gordon Cooper's conversation with mission control from a 'Mercury' spacecraft on May 15-16, 1963, and that similar 'alien voices', speaking clearly in what appeared to be a structured language, were picked up by 'Apollo 8' astronauts orbiting the Moon in December 1968. But it is hard to take seriously those who claim to be in regular touch with E.T.I.s by radio, telepathy or direct personal contact. One of the largest and best known of such organizations is the London-based Aetherius Society, founded in 1955 by George King (b.1919). King and his followers claim to guard Earth against evil E.T.I.s with the aid of the 'Cosmic Masters' (who include Jesus, the Buddha and a Martian scientist) and the Saturn-based 'Interplanetary Parliament'.

American astronaut Gordon Cooper: some claim 'voices' that broke in on his talk with mission control while orbiting Earth in a 'Mercury' spacecraft were those of the crew of an alien spaceship from the constellation of Boötes.

While circling the Moon, the 'Apollo 8' astronauts are also said to have heard 'alien voices'.

Built by Cornell University in association with the U.S. Department of Defense, the world's most powerful radio telescope at Arecibo, Puerto Rico, will play a major part in N.A.S.A.'s 'alien hunt' of the 1990s.

Ancient astronomers quite accurately estimated inter-planetary distances. Like scientists today, some believed intelligent life might exist on other planets.

❑ In the 19th century believers in E.T.I.s suggested it might be possible to communicate with them via the Sahara Desert. It was proposed enormous geometrical figures be dug there – but to be visible from, for example, Mars, even with modern telescopes, they would have needed to be some 645km (400mi) across. Some suggested that huge fires in the shape of 'universal' geometric concepts like the Pythagorean theorem might be lit in the Sahara. French inventor Charles Cros (1842-88) advocated construction of a giant mirror to flash messages to Mars.

❑ In November 1974 scientists at Arecibo Observatory, Puerto Rico, used the world's most powerful radio telescope, with a 305m (1000ft) bowl, to beam a 3-minute message a distance of c.22,500 light years to the globular star cluster Messier 13 in the constellation of Hercules. But even if alien beings there are capable of decoding the signal, no one expects an early reply: the message will not arrive until c.A.D. 25,000.

❑ There have been reports of U.F.O.s seen by astronauts in space. Orbiting Earth in 'Gemini 4' in 1965, James McDivitt saw an object 'with big arms' at c.15km (25mi) distance. The photographs he took were unaccountably lost – and McDivitt claimed that some later published were fakes. N.A.S.A. attributed the sighting to optical illusion.

Aliens under water

Ufologists are undecided whether Unidentified Submarine Objects (U.S.O.s) – strange craft seen in or above the waters covering nearly three-quarters of Earth's surface – are U.F.O.s with submarine capabilities, or separate phenomena. Some suggest they may be from an unknown, undersea civilization, even from lost Atlantis. Some say extra-terrestrials have undersea bases in the South Atlantic off Argentina, where there have been so many U.S.O. reports since 1959, when an 'enormous, fish-shaped craft' was spotted in Buenos Aires harbour, that local people refer to 'Martian bases' as established fact. Earlier U.S.O.s favoured the Persian Gulf, where in c.1840-1910 there were a dozen well attested sightings of silent, luminous, revolving 'wheels', up to 40m (130ft) in diameter. In 1946 there were more than 1,000 reports of craft entering or leaving Scandinavian lakes. It was suggested the 'ghost rockets' were Soviet missiles on test – but the missile programme was then in its infancy, and no wreckage was found to support the view. Commonsense says craft seen entering the water may be crashing aircraft or mis-sightings of heavenly bodies low on the horizon. Those seen emerging may be submarine-launched missiles – or simply flocks of seabirds taking off. Many U.S.O.s located underwater by electronic means are likely to be mundane submarines on clandestine missions – like the 50 or more contacts a year made up to the 1990s by the Swedish military with what were almost certainly Soviet submarines. But not all: off Puerto Rico in 1963 the carrier *Wasp* and 12 other U.S. warships tracked an underwater contact for four days, registering speeds of up to 280kmh (175mph) and depths exceeding 8,230m (27,000ft) – some four times the capabilities of any terrestrial submersible.

A scientist investigates the bottom of Lake Kölmjärv, northern Sweden, one of the many sites of reported 'ghost rocket' or U.S.O. 'landings' or 'take-offs' in Scandinavia in 1946.

Discreet testing of equipment meant for clandestine warfare is a possible source of U.S.O. reports. Here, members of a U.S. Navy 'SEALs' underwater demolition team ride a swimmer delivery vehicle.

French novelist Jules Verne anticipated modern U.S.O. scares – and the powers of today's submarines – in Captain Nemo's sinister Nautilus of *Twenty Thousand Leagues Under the Sea* (1870).

FACT FILE

❏ A very early mention of a U.S.O. occurs in a medieval Japanese chronicle, which describes how a strange craft shaped like a drum, about 6m (20ft) in diameter, emerged from the Inland Sea in 1361.

❏ One of the best atttested U.S.O. sightings took place at Amapa, northern Brazil, in November 1980. At least 70 persons at a ferry landing on the Araguari River saw a 'solid object', some 4.6m (15ft) around, emerge from the water, hover at between 6-183m (20-600ft) for some 4 minutes, coming within 30m (100ft) of the watchers, and then move slowly towards the sea.

❏ Although most reports of U.S.O.s are of large craft, one seen at the mouth of the Pascagoula River, Miss., on November 6, 1973, was more like a pesky insect. Fishermen alerted Coast Guards to a 'stainless steel' U.S.O, only some 0.9m (3ft) long and c.10cm (4in) broad. Flashing an amber light, it buzzed their boats for nearly an hour, evading attempts to swat it with oars.

❏ Jim and Coral Lorenzen, who in 1952 founded America's Aerial Phenomena Research Organization (A.P.R.O.), have stated that U.S.O.s are 'mapping and mining craft' launched from U.F.O.s by extra-terrestrials intent on exploiting the minerals beneath Earth's oceans.

The Earth is flat . . .

Most ancient peoples assumed Earth was a flat disc, floating on a great ocean or supported by gigantic beings, like Atlas of Greek myth. Early Christians accepted Flat Earthism: some fundamentalists still do, arguing that the books of *Isaiah* and *Revelations* refer to 'the four corners of the Earth'. From the 6th century A.D., when the *Christian Topography* of Cosmas of Alexandria said Earth was a rectangular plane centred on Jerusalem and separated from Paradise by a surrounding ocean, Flat Earthism was an article of faith, unquestioned by theologians from St. Augustine to Luther. By the 17th century scientists had convinced most people that Earth is spherical. But some disagree. In Britain the Zetetic Society (Greek: *zeteo*; 'I find out for myself') flourished in the 19th century, 'proving' Flat Earthism by complex measurement experiments in Eastern England's fenlands. America's leading Flat Earthists belonged to the Christian Apostolic Church founded by John Dowie (d.1907), who in 1895 set up a fundamentalist settlement at Zion, Ill. From 1905, under Glenn Wilbur Voliva (d.1942), Zion was a strictly ruled but prosperous community, supporting publications and radio stations through which Voliva spread his beliefs. He taught that the North Pole is the central point of Earth's disc; its circumference is the South Pole, a wall of ice, beyond which lies Hell. Earth is stationary in space; the Sun and Moon are small and only a few hundred miles away. Faced with evidence derived from the space programme, his remaining disciples say the programme is a hoax – set up by the British government, agreed to by President Kennedy and Soviet leader Khruschev at a secret summit, scripted by sci-fi eminence Arthur C. Clarke, and with visual effects faked by Hollywood.

Like others of its kind, the 13th century *Mappa Mundi* ('World Map') now in Hereford Cathedral, England, portrays Earth as a flat disc surrounded by water.

It was axiomatic to mapmakers of the earlier Christian era that Jerusalem, 'Holy City' of the faith, must be situated at the very centre of the Earth.

A sphere in space: Earth as most people now accept it to be. Some Flat Earthists say such evidence from the space programme is faked.

Galileo's perfection of the astronomical telescope in c.1610 enormously advanced humanity's knowledge of the universe.

Galileo (1564-1642) was one of many scientists persecuted for questioning then orthodox religious teachings on the nature of the universe.

FACT FILE

❑ Martin Luther (1483-1546), father of Protestantism, produced a telling argument against those who said Earth was a sphere. It could not be, he said, for if it were, people living 'underneath' would not be able to witness Christ's Second Coming.

❑ Paul Kruger (1825-1904), pillar of the fundamentalist Dutch Reformed Church and leader of South Africa's Transvaal Republic against the British in the Boer War (1899-1902), sailed to Europe to seek support. On the way, the ship's captain, with sextant and telescope, convinced him of Earth's curvature. Kruger, it is said, then threw his *Bible* into the ocean: proved untrue, he declared, it was no longer any use to him.

❑ Glenn Wilbur Voliva became a millionaire from the manufacture of chocolate-covered biscuits – but showed little sweetness in his rule over Zion. Its c.16,000 inhabitants were subjected to a 10 p.m. curfew and forbidden to whistle or sing in public or drive at more than 8kmh (5mph). Alcohol, cigarettes and, for women, makeup, high heels, swimsuits and other 'immodest dress' were banned. The rules were enforced by Voliva's private police force, whose badge was a Dove of Peace with the word 'Patience'. Voliva's reign ended in the later 1930s, after he lost most of his wealth in the Depression.

. . . or is it hollow?

Flat Earthism is of ancient origin; Hollow Earthism dates from the time most people accepted Earth was spherical. Astronomer Edmond Halley (1656-1742) was among the first to theorize that Earth might consist of two or more concentric spheres. Soon arose fantasies of unknown lands peopled by strange races in Earth's interior. In the 1820s John Symmes, a U.S. Army officer, came close to persuading Congress to fund an expedition to the North Pole where, he said, lay an entrance to five inner spheres. His son Americus claimed that one 'gate' had been found in ancient times by the 'lost tribes of Israel': hence their disappearance. Later disciples claimed that the aurorae seen in polar regions were reflections of an 'inner Earth's' Sun on our clouds. In 1909 Admiral Peary reached the North Pole – and, like later Arctic (and Antarctic) travellers, failed to notice a large hole. But Hollow Earthists say no one has ever really been to either pole – they may think they have, but are misled because compasses go haywire within a 240km (150mi) radius of the poles – and claim that dark patches on satellite photographs clearly show large holes in polar regions. Others believe we live not on Earth's surface, but inside it. This was the view of Cyrus Reed Teed ('Koresh') (1839-1908), American healer and alchemist, who from 1894 established a 'New Jersusalem' at Estero, Fla., where he planned a great 'Koreshan' city. He built a 'Rectilineator' apparatus to prove that Earth's surface slopes upward, showing we live within a hollow sphere. Estero declined after his death, but revived after 1945 when its land holdings in coastal Florida soared in value. Today it is reported to be a flourishing community dedicated to 'green' principles – reflecting Teed's own pioneer interest in ley lines and 'magnetic Earth energy'.

A projection based on satellite photography shows the Antarctic 'ozone hole'. Hollow Earthists say a real hole ('gate') opens there too.

In the 1930s Hollow Earthists hoped pioneer rocket engineer Wernher von Braun would aid their cause – but he appears to be 'seeing through it' in 1958!

Cyrus Reed Teed ('Koresh': Hebrew for 'Cyrus') and his helpmate Annie Ordway ('Victoria Gratia') relax in the luxurious surroundings of the Founder's House at his 'New Jerusalem' at Estero, Florida, in the late 1890s.

❏ Germany's anti-Semitic Nazi party encouraged the exploration of Flat and Hollow Earth theories – because if proved true they would discredit the orthodox 'Jewish science' of Albert Einstein and others. In 1933 the city council at Magdeburg decided to find out whether we live inside a Hollow Earth by sending up rockets – which might travel in a direct line to Australia. Modern rocketry was in its infancy and few got off the ground, but the experiments helped inspire research that led to Germany's fearsome missiles of World War II. Among the scientists at Magdeburg was Wernher von Braun (1912-77), later a creator of the U.S. space programme.

❏ U.S. sage Alfred Lawson, a former aeronautical engineer, founded a University of Lawsonomy at Des Moines, Iowa, in the 1950s. He believed not only that Earth is hollow, but that it is alive: a primitive life form with the North Pole as its mouth – and the South Pole as its anus. He also taught that the human brain is operated by tiny living creatures – menorgs (good) and disorgs (bad) – a theory pioneered, he said, by the inventor Edison (below).

Riddles in rocks

Science has solved prehistoric puzzles once thought supernatural. We now know 'dragons' bones' for dinosaur fossils, 'elfshot' for Stone Age weapons and 'giants' graves' for ancient human burial chambers. But some mysteries – like human footprints in stones much older than the first humans – remain. In rocks at Glen Rose, Tex., tracks of humans and dinosaurs (extinct more than 60 million years before humans evolved) run side by side. Some are fakes, made for sale in the Depression: but locals swear they were inspired by real ones – and researchers in 1976 found more, in inaccessible underwater sites. Humans have existed for less than 2,000,000 years, and have worn shoes for a fraction of that time – but in 1927 a fossil hunter in Nevada found the print of a leather shoe (with stitching finer than the average modern shoemaker's) in limestone c.180-225,000,000 years old. In 1968 Antelope Spring, Utah, yielded a similar puzzle: a trilobite (a small marine species extinct for 280,000,000 years) embedded in the print of a sandaled foot. Human artifacts have been found embedded in solid rock: nails, gold thread, tools and an 18th century French stonemason's complete kit. Blasting work at Dorchester, Mass., in 1851 freed a rockbound, fragile metal vase – so fine it was said to be the work of Tubal-cain, Biblical father of metallurgy. In 1969 a geode (hollow stone) said to be 500,000 years old was cut open to reveal a metal shaft with white ceramic casing that looked like a modern spark plug. There are hundreds of reports of people breaking open stones to find a live toad in a snug, toad-shaped cavity. No one has explained how they get there, or how they survive without air, food or water. Scientists no longer think they were trapped in mud at the time of the Flood or even the Creation – but have yet to produce a better explanation.

19th century quarry workers break open a stone and find a live toad within. Many such cases are reported; scientists disagree whether they are folklore, hoaxes or baffling fact.

Perhaps entombed toads get air or moisture through cracks in the rock; or perhaps they survive in suspended animation. But how does a toad get into its rocky hole in the first place?

❏ The puzzle of entombed toads has inspired some cruel experiments. One subject, a horned toad nicknamed Old Rip, was walled up in a cavity in a new courthouse at Eastland, Tex., in 1897. When the building was demolished in 1928 crowds came to see if the toad had survived. It had – but died a year later, worn out perhaps by the demands of fame and a nationwide tour, including a visit to the White House to meet President Coolidge.

❏ In 1932 gold prospectors in the Pedro Mountains of Wyoming found a human mummy only 36cm (14in) tall (above). X-rays proved it was a real human body, apparently of advanced age. Speculation sprang up of a lost tribe of miniature Native Americans. In 1979 new studies of the X-rays led to a reassessment: it now seems likely 'Pedro' was a deformed prehistoric infant or foetus. Further study is frustrated: the mummy disappeared in 1950.

Fossil tracks by the Paluxy River near Glen Rose, Tex., look very human – though one theory ascribes them to a small, two-legged dinosaur trailing its toes in the mud.

Alongside run the larger tracks of a three-toed dinosaur. If the small tracks are accepted as human, then geologists have a major problem – or time travel is a reality.

Signs of ill omen?

To our ancestors, who saw signs from Heaven in the sky, comets foretold 'famine or pestilence or war or the destruction of the Earth by fearful means'. Halley's Comet, seen every 76 years, was blamed for all manner of disasters, and in 1456 was condemned by Pope Callixtus as an agent of the Devil. But omens can be read two ways. A visit from Halley's Comet before the battle of Hastings in 1066 heralded English defeat – but for victor William the Conqueror it was a case of 'A new star: a new king.' That same belief inspired the Wise Men who, St. Matthew says, followed a star to the Holy Child in Bethlehem. The Star in the East remains a mystery to astronomers, though it too may have been a comet – or a nova, aurora or planetary conjunction. Another comet may have caused the 'Tunguska Event', a mystery explosion that shook the world on June 30, 1908. At Tunguska, Siberia, peasants saw the sky 'open to the ground and fire pour out', devastating an area of c.2,000sq km (770sq mi), killing livestock, and flattening forests and buildings. The blast was heard 800km (500mi) away; shock waves registered as far off as Washington, D.C.; and over Europe a burning crimson sky made midnight bright as noon. Tunguska's remoteness delayed serious investigation until 1927, when Soviet scientist Leonid Kulik began a 20-year inquiry which raised more questions than it answered. Whatever hit Tunguska left no material traces like craters or meteorite fragments, but caused radiation burns on livestock and genetic mutations in local plants and animals – suggesting an atomic blast on a scale far beyond that seen 37 years later at Hiroshima. Some blame the Tunguska explosion on a comet which vaporized in the Earth's atmosphere – or on a 'black hole' in space, 'anti-matter', or even the crash of an alien spaceship.

In ancient times, stones that fell from the sky were often worshipped. This one, in South Africa, is still an object of awe to scientists: at c.60 tonnes it is the heaviest meteorite yet found.

The 'Tunguska incident' in 1908 flattened forests for miles around. This picture was taken in 1929, 7km (4.3mi) from the centre.

'A new star: a new king.' The Bayeux Tapestry depiction of the Norman Conquest of England shows Halley's Comet bringing defeat to English King Harold in 1066.

A million-tonne meteorite hit Arizona 20,000 years ago harder than a 30 megaton H-bomb. Meteor Crater, 1.6km (1mi) wide and 174m (570ft) deep, was blasted out by its impact.

❑ Some 100 million meteors hurtle towards Earth every day (above), but disintegrate into dust before arriving. Most are only pinhead size to start with. Sometimes large fragments fall to Earth as meteorites, but even these are small cause for alarm. A 4kg (9lb) meteorite which smashed through the roof of an Alabama housewife and struck her only bruised her arm and hip – and gave her the distinction of being the only human on record to have been hit by a meteorite.

❑ Centuries ago, the Inuit of Greenland developed iron tools despite not knowing how to smelt iron. Unlike most peoples, they had a stock of near-pure iron to hand: three large meteorites which had conveniently fallen on their land in ancient times. Today one of them, weighing 34 tonnes, is on display in New York's Hayden Planetarium.

❑ Archaeologists excavating a Mexican temple found a meteorite wrapped in mummy clothes.

Corpse-candles, goblins and 'Merry Dancers'

A rare photograph, taken in Austria in 1978, of the elusive and eccentric ball lightning – a luminous globe that does not act like lightning at all.

Modern science can explain most of Nature's firework displays. Our ancestors thought lights flickering over marshland were 'corpse-candles' borne by lost souls, or goblins' lanterns – Will o' the Wisp, Jack o' Lantern, Kit Candlestick – luring travellers into bogs. Now we know the *ignis fatuus* ('foolish fire') is just burning marsh gas from rotting plants. Electrical storms at sea can create 'fire' that plays along ships' upperworks: St. Elmo's fire (from St. Erasmus, patron of seamen), or corposant ('holy body'). Most spectacular is the aurora: bands of coloured light in the sky, usually seen in high latitudes – hence the name 'Northern Lights'. (The Southern Hemisphere has its *Aurora Australis*, or 'Southern Lights'.) In Norse folklore the aurora shone from the golden shields of Valkyries, warrior maidens who led souls to Valhalla. France calls the lights *les chèvres dansantes*, 'dancing goats'; Britain knows them as 'the Merry Dancers'; in Celtic tales they are the *Fir Chlis* – fairy fighters whose blood stains the sky and falls as red pebbles, 'blood stones'. Scientists ascribe the Northern Lights to electrically charged solar particles striking Earth's magnetic field – but they cannot explain ball lightning. For years they denied its existence: now they say this rare type of lightning in the form of a luminous sphere denies all laws of physics. Lightning balls may enter houses by closed doors or windows and 'explore' the interior with erratic movements: they spin, hover or bounce, without burning what they touch. Soon they may slip out as mysteriously as they came – or explode. Such explosions melt metal, kill beasts or blow up fuel stores – but rarely hurt people. A woman who brushed a lightning ball away got a sore hand – and a scorched skirt where the ball exploded. Some say ball lightning acts as if it has a mind of its own, displaying playful curiosity.

Folk traditions ascribe the shimmering lights and colours of the *Aurora Borealis*, or 'Northern Lights', to the activities of Otherworld beings – shieldmaidens or fairy warriors – in the sky.

A spectacle literally 'out of this world': an expanse of the *Aurora Australis* ('Southern Lights') photographed by astronauts on the space shuttle 'Atlantis' while orbiting Earth.

Fire from Heaven

Late at night on May 25, 1985, teenager Paul Hayes was walking down a quiet road in London when he burst into flames. Enveloped in fire from the waist up, he thought he must die – but 30 seconds later the flames vanished as inexplicably as they began. With badly burned hands, arms and head, Paul was one of the rare survivors of a phenomenon reported some 200 times since the 1600s: spontaneous human combustion. Most victims burn to death in an unnaturally intense fire of unknown source, eerily localized in a small area. As in Paul's case, it strikes suddenly – victims rarely have time to call for aid – and without apparent external source: sufferers seem to self-ignite. The fire can reduce a body to ashes more quickly than a crematorium. Yet little else is touched: clothes over charred bones, or a bed under a cremated body, may remain unburnt. When Mrs. Mary Reeser burnt up in her Florida apartment in 1951, nothing was left of the 79kg (175lb) woman but 4.5kg (10lb) of ash, a shrunken skull, a charred liver – and an unburnt foot still in a satin slipper. So fierce a fire should have destroyed the apartment, but it was limited to a small circle: the victim's habit of sitting with a leg outstretched had preserved her foot. Forensic scientist and fire death specialist Dr. Milton Krogman found it all unaccountable: 'As I review it, the short hairs on my neck bristle with vague fear. Were I living in the Middle Ages, I'd mutter something about black magic.' A rational explanation is hard to find. Victorian doctors blamed drink. Victims, they said, were drunks who had imbibed so much alcohol they became inflammable – a view the temperance movement welcomed. Modern theories include excessively flatulent innards, static electricity, high-frequency sound and microwave radiation – but all fail to explain how these might work.

Mrs. Mary Reeser was reduced to ashes, yet the fire hardly touched her apartment. The local Police Chief commented: 'this . . . just couldn't have happened, but it did'.

A movie stuntman dares the flames with fireproof gear and helpers to hand – but spontaneous combustion has no such escape clauses.

A 1966 victim of spontaneous combustion was retired Pennsylvania physician Dr. John Bentley. Intense heat reduced his body to fine ashes and burned through the floor beneath him – yet spared most of the room, his walking frame and half his right leg.

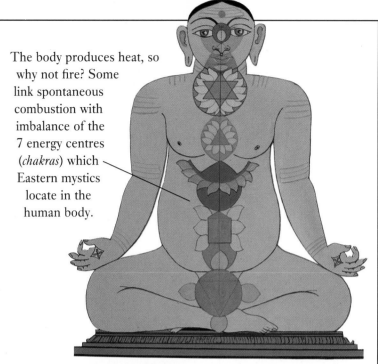

The body produces heat, so why not fire? Some link spontaneous combustion with imbalance of the 7 energy centres (*chakras*) which Eastern mystics locate in the human body.

FACT FILE

❏ In 1725 French innkeeper Jean Millet was condemned to death for murdering his wife, found burnt to ashes in her kitchen. Luckily for Millet, trainee surgeon Claude-Nicolas Le Cat, a guest at the inn, realized this was no normal fire. It had almost consumed the woman's body and burnt the floor under her – but nothing else. Le Cat was so struck by this unnatural effect that he persuaded the court to change its verdict from murder to 'visitation of God'.

❏ Spontaneous combustion usually limits itself to humans and objects: animals seem exempt. A possible exception was Hayes, a retriever pup which caught fire by its home in Jarrow, England, in 1978. Hearing yelps, owner Jean Payne looked out of the window to see her dog 'with flames leaping up from his belly'. The police assumed a case of human sadism; but no one was seen, and flesh does not normally catch fire so easily. (Hayes survived his ordeal to make a full recovery.)

❏ Fires sometimes break out for no apparent cause in houses afflicted with poltergeist activity, a phenomenon that may be connected with spontaneous human combustion. Researchers also note cases of 'fire-prone' individuals, in whose presence fires repeatedly break out – but are not, apparently, deliberately caused by them.

Cereal stories

Farmers who find crops crushed by trespassers are justifiably annoyed. But – in England at least – if corn (U.S.: wheat) is flattened in a symmetrical circle, neither careless picnickers nor alfresco lovers are likely to be blamed. Media reports over the past decade identify such effects as 'crop circles' – although the irate farmer may not know whether to blame freak winds, hoaxers, or U.F.O.s. Crop circles have been in the news since the early 1980s, when most reports came from southern England, but still remain a mystery. Unlike typical cases of careless or wilful damage, the crop is flattened in a precise design: usually a single ring, sometimes with a curved or straight 'tail', sometimes multiple rings, sometimes linear patterns. The stalks are not broken, only bent over at the base. Still commonest in England, crop circles are known also in the U.S.A., Australia, Canada, France and Japan. They seem to be a 20th century phenomenon; although an English report of 1678 told of a field of oats mysteriously 'mown' overnight in circles – 'as if the Devil had a mind to shew his

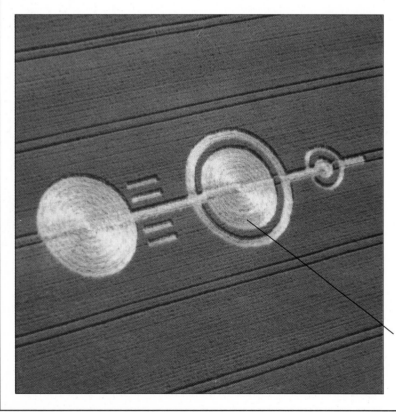

dexterity in the art of husbandry'. Today we are more likely to blame strange occurrences on space aliens than on Old Nick, and some Ufologists identify the circles as 'flying saucer' landing sites, or 'U.F.O. nests'. Other theories include secret military devices, sportive hedgehogs and hoaxers. Some circles are admitted fakes – at least one complex example was instigated by a tabloid newspaper – but it is difficult to believe in teams of hoaxers working worldwide over so many years. Most scientists say freak weather conditions are the cause: Dr. Terence Meaden of the British Tornado and Storm Research Organisation suggests an electrically charged atmospheric vortex, formed when air passes over certain landscape features.

Crop circles are reported worldwide, but most appear in the 'Wessex corridor' (Hampshire and Wiltshire) of southern England. This impressive triplet group appeared on July 13, 1990, at Crawley Down, Hampshire.

It is hard to believe that such elaborate and symmetrical geometric patterns as this July 1991 example from Banbury Castle, Wiltshire, are accidents of nature.

In August 1678 a crop of oats in Hertfordshire, England, was mysteriously mown in rings. Ascribed to a 'Mowing Devil', was this the first recorded crop circle?

Prehistoric 'cup and ring' marks carved in rocks in north Britain puzzle scholars – but some researchers link the patterns with crop circles.

Hoaxers and serious students of crop circles can produce pretty convincing crop circles like these made at East Kennett, Wiltshire, in July 1991.

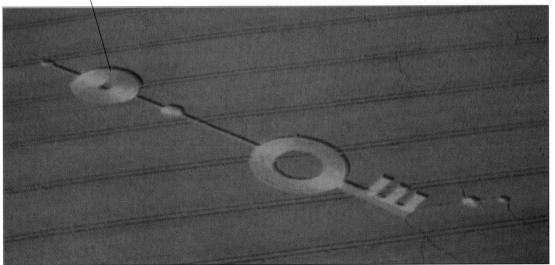

FACT FILE

❏ In July 1992 the 'Masters of the Cereal Universe' (a three man team from Yeovil, Devon) made a fake crop circle – and won £3,000 ($5,400). They were overall winners from 12 teams who competed in the world's first crop circle competition, held in Buckinghamshire, England. The event was designed to enable serious researchers into circles to study the techniques used by hoaxers.

❏ Some see crop circles as a modern psychic phenomenon, for they are often linked with strange lights in the sky and similar occurrences, and tend to occur near ancient monuments. Some researchers think they respond to human thoughts, rather like poltergeists. On several occasions publication of a new crop circle theory has been swiftly followed by the appearance of a circle that contradicts it. On the day Dr. Meaden (below) published his vortex theory, based on the direction in which cornstalks swirl within a circle, a new crop circle appeared – swirling in the 'wrong' way.

Strange rains

It never really 'rains cats and dogs', as the saying goes; but apparently it does sometimes 'rain' other animals – and vegetables and minerals. In old times folk saw edible rains – of grain or shellfish – as 'manna from heaven', while rains of 'blood' literally put the fear of God into them. Today we explain such strange rains as the result of freak wind conditions, and know that 'showers of blood' are only red sand or insect droppings. Harder to explain away are accounts of animals falling from the sky – typically in large numbers of the same species, size and age. Fish or frogs are the commonest of these uncommon rains; lizards, snails, mice and insects are also recorded. Some are dead, like the eels which fell on Hendon, England, in 1918 (providing cartloads of fertilizer), or the stinking, headless fish which hit Jelalpur, India, in 1830. But many reach the ground alive and wriggling, apparently unharmed by the fall. Sceptics ascribe 'frog rains' to the over-active imaginations of people who see frogs hopping about during rainstorms, and 'fish rains' to hoaxers throwing buckets of river water. But faced with reliable eyewitness accounts, others seek explanations. 17th century scientists thought fish or frogs might be birthed in the sky by 'spontaneous generation', and then fall to earth; today's theory is that freak whirlwinds or waterspouts draw up creatures from one spot to drop them elsewhere. Student of odd events Charles Fort (1874-1932) thought the only explanation to fit the facts was teleportation: a natural force transporting objects instantaneously through space. As he argued, no one can explain how a whirlwind could deposit its living load undamaged – or pick up a a few thousand well-matched fish with no other water creatures, mud or detritus.

Patrolman James Johnstone holds a steel chain which fell from the sky across a tractor driven by Wallace Baker at Rock Hill, Mo., on May 15, 1959.

A 1658 woodcut depicts a 'fall of fish, or rain of fish from the skies' – a phenomenon first recorded in the early third century A.D. by Greek scholar Athenaeus.

Most 'animal showers' comprise a 'matched set' of beasts of identical size and age, like these fish which fell on East Ham, London, England, in May 1984.

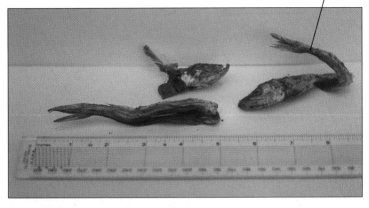

Charles Fort saw teleportation as a force which once moved mountains or dispersed species round the world, and now just toys with frogs and small fry.

A 'frog rain' depicted on the cover of *Fate* magazine, May 1958. It was once thought little frogs hatched out in the air from wind-borne frogspawn, to fall to earth in a 'shower'.

FACT FILE

❑ In 1821 a rain of snails on a farm in Avon, England, was held to be divine punishment for the farmer's 'disrespect to the virtues of our late Queen' (Caroline, wife of King George IV: according to historians she had very little virtue).

❑ In 1934 U.S. Navy airship *Macon* was flying over California when the crew heard a loud splash over their heads. Investigating, they found a 0.6m (2ft) alligator 'swimming around excitedly' in a water-filled ballast bag. It could have been worse: an alligator that landed with 'a thud and a grunt' outside a California home in 1964 was 1.5m (5ft) long.

❑ A Greek writer of c.A.D.200 recorded a remarkably heavy rain of frogs in Paeonia and Dardinia which drove locals to despair. Their homes were full of frogs; they found boiled or roasted frogs in their dinners and live frogs in their drinks. In the end, 'annoyed also by the smell of those that died, they fled the country'.

❑ In the 1950s naturalist Sally Carrighar studied lemmings in Alaska. Tracks started from nowhere in shallow snow as if the animals had fallen from the sky; some began faintly as if they had coasted down. She found no natural explanation for this – or for the disappearance of captive specimens from a secure pen. But Inuit call lemmings 'mice from the sky' and say they fall to Earth from a star.

Wild children

In 1920 missionary Joseph Singh went ghost hunting in the Indian jungle. He led a party to dig out the lair of half human, half beast 'man ghosts' reported by the people of Midnapore. What he found was three wolves guarding a strange family – two wolf cubs and two human 'ghosts': dirty, snarling, little girls who seemed to think they were wolves. He took the children, whom he named Amala and Kamala, to an orphanage, where they acted like wild beasts. They ran on calloused knees and elbows, could not stand upright, use their hands or talk, and ate only raw meat. Amala, the younger, survived only a few months; Kamala lived eight years more, learning a few human skills and some 30 words. These 'wolf children of Midnapore' were not unique. Legend says Romulus and Remus, founders of Rome, were raised by a wolf; a 'wolf boy' was captured in Germany in 1344; others last century in India; and a 'monkey boy' in Sri Lanka in 1973. Like Amala, such children rarely live long after capture; although an Indian boy stolen by a wolf in 1843 and later restored to his family survived to return to the jungle in 1851. Sceptics say young children cannot survive in the wild: they believe 'wolf children' are retarded youngsters abandoned by their parents and later found, by chance, in close proximity to animals – when their abnormal behaviour is attributed to animal upbringing. They may be right. But many animals, including wolves, show innate compassion for youngsters of any species. In 1982 charity workers in the slums of Manila, Philippines, took an orphan child from a mongrel bitch said to have adopted him more than a year earlier, suckling him like her own pup and driving off would-be rescuers. They reported 2-year-old Joel acted just like a dog.

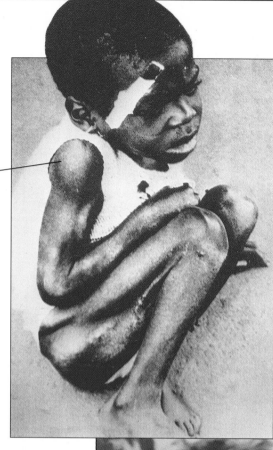

This boy, captured in Uganda in 1986, was said to have been living with a family of apes. He lacked speech and apparently feared humans.

'The wild boy of Aveyron' was captured in his late teens in France last century, living like a wild animal. He was eventually taught to walk upright and speak a few words, but remained severely subnormal until he died, aged about 40.

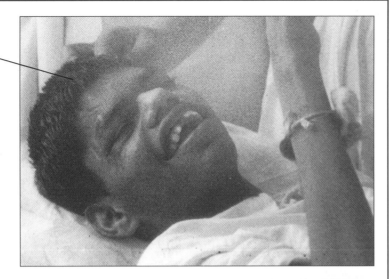

A modern 'wolf boy', Ramu was found in the Indian jungle, playing with two wolf cubs, in 1960. His finders believed he had been raised by wolves: sceptics reject the idea.

'Wild children' show no sign of human socialization. But is their abnormal conduct learnt from animals, or merely disturbed behaviour caused by brain-damage and increased by parental neglect?

❏ While scientists argued whether Amala and Kamala were really raised by wolves, theologians debated with equal heat whether they had souls. Many thought they had not, since they had lived as animals and failed to develop normal human minds.

❏ In 1963 French anthropologist Jean-Claude Armen reported a 'gazelle boy' (above) – a 10-year-old child living with wild gazelles in the Sahara. He acted as one of the herd, communicating with sniffs and licks and sharing their diet of roots (which had worn his teeth level like theirs). He also ran like a gazelle: Armen estimated his speed above 48kmh (30mph), which would leave champion sprinter Carl Lewis, who covers 100m at c.37kmh (23mph), standing.

Numerate nags and complaining cats

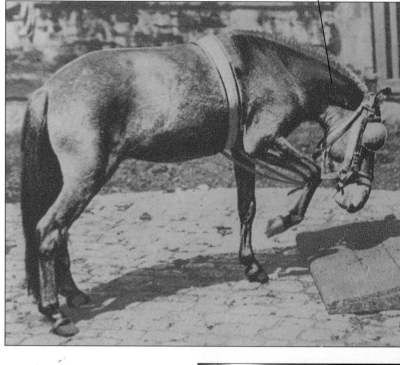

Clever Hans began by learning numbers from rows of skittles, and went on to demonstrate advanced maths and reading. Here he spells out his name.

Christmas Eve once saw children hiding in stables to eavesdrop on talking animals – an annual miracle said to occur to honour the beasts at the Bethlehem crib. More sinister were the talking 'familiars' (demons in animal form) attributed to witches; in the 16th century John Banks was charged with witchcraft when he claimed his performing horse Marocco could talk. Scholars said animals might acquire speech: in 1661 diarist Samuel Pepys, impressed by a baboon which 'understood much English', thought it capable of learning speech or sign language. Some 300 years later scientists took up the idea. Since the 1960s apes have been trained to 'talk' with humans via symbols or sign language – but not speech, for which apes' voiceboxes are ill-suited. Outside the laboratory, such attempts appeared earlier. In the early 1900s Wilhelm von Osten taught a horse, Clever Hans, sign language, maths, reading and musical appreciation. Early investigators compared Hans to 'an intelligent 14-year-old boy'. Academics rubbished these claims; but when von Osten died, Hans continued his schooling with a string of learned nags owned by Karl Krall of Elberfeld, Germany. The Elberfeld horses baffled researchers with complex feats – but whether such animals use reasoning power, have psychic gifts, or are just well-trained circus performers is still fiercely debated. A few beasts are reported to use human speech: Batir, a Russian zoo elephant, is said to have some 20 phrases, from 'Batir is good' to 'Have you watered the elephant?' Cats and dogs are reported to have said things like 'I love you', or 'I want a biscuit' – and Whitey, a Florida tomcat of the 1960s, sounds positively human. Speaking in a 'whining, self-pitying manner', he used his gift to express dislike of other cats, accuse a neighbour of hitting him, and moan 'Why no one love me?'

In the 1500s, when performing horse Marocco told numbers on a pair of dice, people called it witchcraft: today most put it down to a skilful trainer.

An investigatory committee found Hans performed just as well in his teacher's absence.

Some class 'educated animals' with circus performers like these 'liberty horses'. Others are convinced they use their own brain power to think, calculate and communicate.

We are always ready to 'humanize' animals. In 1986 Morris the cat stood as a Democratic candidate for the U.S. presidency – and scored high in popularity polls.

❏ Many parrots (below) mimic human speech, but do not understand what they say. But in the 1980s one called Alex was reported to have gone beyond 'parroting' speech. At Purdue University, Ind., Alex learned to link words with objects (mostly food and toys), and went on to express simple thoughts in speech. He asked for objects by name – and said moulting depressed him.

❏ In the 1960s English setter Arli learned to operate the keys of a giant typewriter with his nose to produce messages like 'arli go car', or 'be good dog get ball and go bed'. 50 years earlier, Airedale terrier Rolf put on a more sophisticated performance. Using a paw-tap code, he solved maths questions – and showed a certain wit. When a woman asked how to please him, he told her: 'Wag your tail.'

❏ When gorilla Koko was taught sign language, she promptly used it to ask for a kitten of her own. In June 1984, she was presented with a kitten and signed 'Love that', to her trainers. She adored her pet, which she named All Ball, describing it as 'soft good cat' and signing to it just as human pet owners talk to their pets.

Nazca Lines: art for aeronauts

A page from the Nazca picture book: a giant spider, c.45m (148ft) long. The shallow lines scraped in the soil have been preserved by the still, dry desert air.

The aircraft had to be invented before we could appreciate the Nazca Indians' art. Between 400 B.C. and A.D. 600 this mysterious people turned Peru's Nazca desert into a giant picture book. They scraped in the soil huge birds and animals, each drawn in a continuous, fluid line, and c.13,000 straight lines, some over 40km(25mi) long. But none is apparent from ground level: the Nazca Lines were spotted from the air in 1927. Their purpose is a puzzle. Perhaps they were astronomical pointers; but a 1968 study concluded: 'Astronomically speaking, the system is random.' Ufologists see them as 'runways' for alien spacecraft; but the soft ground led researcher Maria Reiche to dismiss the idea: 'The spacemen would have gotten stuck.' Some, admiring their 'modern minimalist' style, see the Nazca drawings as art for art's sake. A 'birth control theory' claims they were made just to occupy a large labour force and thus keep down the population! But a religious function is most likely. Andean Indians still 'walk lines' for spiritual reasons in rituals dating back to the Incas: perhaps the Nazca had such rites. Drawings of water animals (frog, cormorant, duck, killer whale) may have been rain-bringing magic. How the lines were made also intrigues scholars. Ufologists insist it took extraterrestrial intelligence. Research suggests the Nazca worked out their designs on dirt 'drawing boards' some 2m (6ft) square, then plotted out full-scale versions with cords strung between wooden posts. Pondering the fact that Nazca artists could not have seen their work from the ground, American businessman Jim Woodman decided they must have flown over it in hot air balloons, and built one from 'primitive' materials to make his point. But his project showed only that the Nazca could have mastered flight; not that they did.

The Nazca Lines run perfectly straight for miles, regardless of terrain. Many cross each other to form complex networks of triangles, rectangles and trapezoids.

Ufologists seeking evidence that the Nazca Lines relate to visitors from outer space claim this Peruvian rock drawing of a figure with a halo – probably a god – shows an 'ancient astronaut' in a space helmet.

Ancient landscape art may be worked in rocks as well as soil. This Arizona 'medicine wheel' was picked out in boulders for ritual purposes.

The first aerial study of the Nazca Lines was made in 1940 by American Paul Kosok.

Monuments of the Mound Builders

Moundville, Ala., boasts the tallest surviving U.S. temple mound – an earth version of the stone temple pyramids of Central and South America.

American pioneers moving west in the 1780s were puzzled to find thousands of imposing earthen mounds. Some – like Monk's Mound, Ill., 30m (100ft) high and covering 6.5ha (16 acres) – were like the bases of Egyptian pyramids. Others were sculpted into the shapes of giant birds, bears or reptiles. Clearly they were monuments of a major culture. But who were the Mound Builders? Local Native Americans were simple hunters, whom white settlers would not associate with such 'stupendous and wonderful' works. They theorized a lost civilization the Native Americans had destroyed: perhaps one founded by Egyptians, Greeks, Romans, Phoenicians or Danes – even by a race of giants, the lost tribes of Israel or colonists from Atlantis. No one believed Native Americans who said their ancestors built the mounds. In the 1840s a shaman, De-coo-dah, explained: 'The face of the Earth is the red man's book, and those mounds and embankments are some of his letters.' But it took a government survey 40 years later to persuade scholars he spoke truly. We now know the Mound Builders comprised not one but three Native American cultures: Adena (1000 B.C.-A.D.200), Hopewell (300 B.C.-A.D.700) and Mississippian (A.D. 700-c.1550). Many Adena and Hopewell mounds were built as chiefs' tombs; Mississippian mounds were temple platforms. But the great animal sculptures remain a mystery. They are certainly of ritual significance, perhaps – as De-coo-dah claimed – astronomical. Most were built by Hopewell peoples, but the best known is Adena work: the Great Serpent Mound in Ohio, a 405m (1,330ft) snake whose gaping jaws reach for the 'egg' of a smaller mound. The Mound Builders' civilization endured until Spanish conquerors came in 1539 to wipe out their culture. Only their earthen monuments remained to awe later generations.

19th century shaman De-coo-dah described effigy mounds – earth sculptures in geometric, animal or human shape – as symbols of heavenly bodies in which the gods were secretly entombed.

The wealth of grave goods in Adena and Hopewell burial mounds bears witness to a rich culture with a vast trading network. Local craftsmen worked in raw materials imported from across the continent: gold, silver, copper, obsidian, sheets of mica, turtle shells, shark teeth and freshwater pearls.

Some Mississippian mounds were not only platforms for temples but apartment blocks, with dwellings for priests and nobles built on the terraced sides. A house's position indicated the resident's social status. Higher ranks lived higher up the mound, and the chief sometimes built his house on top (see reconstruction above), beside the temple. Commoners made do with ground-level dwellings. This class-consciousness continued among the Mound Builders' descendants, like the Natchez, who maintained a rigid caste system. The upper classes, in descending order, were Suns (royalty), Nobles and Honoured Men and Women (lesser nobles). Commoners were called Stinkards – though not, for courtesy, in their presence.

Best-known of the many Adena earth sculptures, the Great Serpent Mound, Ohio, may commemorate a lunar eclipse. The Moon is shown as the 'egg' which the snake is about to swallow.

A display model demonstrates the structure of the Great Serpent Mound – a colossal work requiring months or years of cooperative labour.

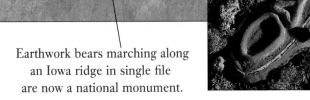

Earthwork bears marching along an Iowa ridge in single file are now a national monument.

Secrets of ancient stones

Through the late Stone and early Bronze Ages (c.3300-1500 B.C.) the peoples of Britain spent much time and effort building nearly 1,000 huge stone monuments, like the stone circles of Stonehenge and Avebury. Historians, scientists, engineers – and cultists – have laboured almost as hard trying to find out why. Some medieval scholars believed Merlin, magical mentor of King Arthur, built Stonehenge; later, popular theory favoured Druids, the Celtic priests whom 18th century romantics credited with mystic powers (but who flourished c.1,000 years after Stonehenge was built). Those who thought the technology beyond Ancient Britons proposed Romans, Phoenicians, Danes, Egyptians, Greeks, Trojans, envoys from the 'lost world' of Atlantis – even Martians. As for the function of stone circles, ideas ranged through cities, temples, cemeteries, schools, trade and social centres, and sports stadiums. The discovery that many stones align with Sun, Moon or major stars gave rise to theories that the stone circles were prehistoric planetariums, observatories, or 'computers' for calculating sunrises, sunsets, lunar cycles and eclipses. Today most scholars agree that astronomical observation was one motive for the erection of circles – but probably not the only one. The scale seems excessive for the one purpose: Stonehenge alone was more than 500 years in building. Some recent discoveries have given new life to the medieval belief that stone circles were raised for (if not by) magical purposes. Dowsers report high magnetic fields and 'corkscrews' of electromagnetic energy (now known to have healing effects) at many sites.

Geiger counters detect natural radioactivity – triggering New Agers' claims that the circles focus beneficial 'earth-energies', and are 'batteries' charged with ancient occult powers.

Begun by late Stone Age farmers, Stonehenge took its final form under wealthy Bronze Age warlords.

Despite this fanciful 19th century view of 'Druid' rites at Stonehenge, its ceremonies remain unknown – but folktales of dancers turned to stone may hark back to ritual dances.

Few modern visitors would agree with scholar Dr. Johnson, who in 1773 dismissed stone circles as not worth visiting, 'for there is neither art nor power in them, and seeing one is quite enough'.

In 1990 dowser Ron Perry tried to cure 'bad vibes' at this standing stone in Powys, Wales, by driving stakes into the soil. Earth acupuncture or archaeological vandalism?

❑ The notion of Stonehenge as an astronomical computer has taken a few knocks. It relies mainly on the alignment of the Heel Stone with Midsummer Day's sunrise – but this alignment is not, and never was, quite accurate. So the temple theory resurfaces. Most recently, Dr. Terence Meaden sees Stonehenge as a vast image of the union of Father God and Mother Goddess. Just after Midsummer sunrise, he points out, the Heel Stone casts a long shadow into the heart of the stone circle – which he sees as an annual picture show of the Sky God's phallus fertilizing the Earth Mother's womb.

❑ A 1991 open air production of Shakespeare's *The Tempest* in a stone circle in Oxfordshire, England, hit problems. Performing among the Rollright Stones (above) (noted among stone circle buffs for high magnetic fields and radiation levels), actors suffered brief memory losses and fainting fits; watches went haywire and power drained from batteries. 'There's no doubt,' the play's director concluded, 'the Rollrights have a strange magnetism.'

Riddle of the stone giants

Recently restored statues once again boast the finishing touch of 'topknots', carved separately from red tufa stone.

In 1722 Dutch Admiral Jacob Roggeveen came upon remote Easter Island in the Pacific Ocean – and a mystery. Huge statues lined the coast: nearly 1,000 stylized figures, 3.6-9m (12-30ft) tall and weighing 12-80 tonnes, with glaring inlaid eyes and red stone 'topknots'. In contrast to the islanders' crude stone tools and unseaworthy canoes (described as 'the worst in the Pacific'), they were clearly monuments of a skilled society. Researchers guessed at a range of ancient races or even visitors from space. But they were indeed, as the islanders themselves always claimed, the work of the Easter Islanders' ancestors. Possibly Polynesians from the western isles, or South Americans from the east, they settled Easter Island in c.A.D.380 to found a unique culture, with a complex picture script (still undeciphered), fine cave art and the famous statues. They prospered for centuries, lining the shore with stone burial platforms (*ahus*) crowned by statues carved from the crater of extinct volcano Rano Raraku. But from c.1600 famine and war – and, later, European slavers' raids – wore them down. Roggeveen, first European to see the statues, was also the last to see worshippers attend them. By 1864 not one statue remained upright; many had lost their heads. Recent studies explain the islanders' decline and the statues' fate. Soil analysis proves the bleak, treeless island was once densely wooded (so much for the idea that its sculptors chose stone for lack of wood). Felled for timber and to clear land for farms and roads, by c.1400 the trees were gone. With them went farmland and fishing grounds: the fertile soil washed away without tree roots to retain it, and there was no timber to build fishing boats. The good life was at an end. Losing faith in their gods, the islanders turned on their statues and felled them.

Today, re-erected statues once again gaze impassively out to sea; but whether they represent gods or mortal chieftains remains a mystery.

Few credited Easter Islanders with the technology to create such colossal statues; but in 1956 explorer Thor Heyerdahl showed how they softened rock with gourds of water and carved with stone tools.

Easter Island's complex *Rapanui* picture script, still undeciphered, is inscribed on tablets known as *Kohau Rongo Rongo*.

Only the vestige of the inlaid eye remains.

Elongated earlobes suggest the statues depict the ancient ruling caste of 'long ears', whose earlobes were stretched with weighted earrings.

FACT FILE

❏ Carvings and paintings (below) of a winged figure adorn rocks and caves – relics of a late (post-1500) Easter Island birdman cult. Each year, when the sooty terns returned from migration, cult followers raced by land and sea to their nesting site on a nearby island, to gather eggs. The one who brought back the first egg won great honour for his clan chief.

❏ Easter Island's sculptural tradition began with dressing stone blocks to face burial platforms, where the dead were interred after the elements and birds cleaned their bones. Later, sculptors turned their skill to statues to crown the platforms. In 1956 explorer Thor Heyerdahl showed how Stone Age tools and techniques served to hew these monuments from solid rock, haul them to their final sites up to four miles away, and erect them.

❏ Easter Islanders tell of two groups of settlers: 'long ears' (whose image may be reflected in the statues' long earlobes) and 'short ears'. They fell into dispute when famine came, the 'short ears' triumphing shortly before Europeans discovered the island.

England's holy hills

Joseph of Arimathaea with the Holy Grail – in Christian legend Christ's cup at the Last Supper, but probably also the sacred cauldron of pagan Celtic religion.

For centuries the town of Glastonbury, Somerset, has been for pagans and Christians alike, as a medieval scholar wrote, 'the holyest erthe in England'. A conical hill, Glastonbury Tor, dominates the landscape. Pagans said it was a gateway to the fairy world, and it was identified with the Isle of Apples or Glass Island of Celtic mythology – and with the Avalon where 'once and future king' Arthur awaits recall. Christian legend says St. Joseph of Arimathaea founded the Abbey under the Tor as Britain's first church. In its 'Chalice Well' he hid the Holy Grail (Jesus's cup at the Last Supper); and there he planted his staff which, as the Glastonbury Thorn, still blooms at Christmas. The Tor itself defied Christianization: an earthquake felled St. Michael's Church on its summit and today only ruins of a later church survive. Ancient Britons' reverence for hills like Glastonbury led them, in c.2750 B.C., to build an artificial one which, modern researchers calculate, cost them more time, labour and wealth than we invest in a space project. Over many years they built up an estimated 35,000,000 basketloads of clay rubble into Silbury Hill in Wiltshire, 40m (130ft) high: Europe's largest manmade mound. Excavations reveal their technical skill, but not their motive. We know Silbury was not a tomb, despite local tales of a royal burial, inspiring treasure hunts from the 18th century onward; nor a fortress, for it lacks defences; and neither site nor design suggests an astronomical observatory. In 1968 a writer suggested it was a beacon 'in a prehistoric system of signalling' – but there are three taller, natural hills nearby. It is almost certainly a sacred site: an extreme view, held by archaeologist Michael Dames, is that Silbury is a vast earth sculpture of the Mother Goddess.

Legend said Silbury Hill, long thought a king's tomb, held a solid gold statue of a horse and rider; but treasure hunters were disappointed.

Christian tradition honours the Glastonbury Thorn, a winter-flowering hawthorn, as a relic of Joseph of Arimathaea.

The ruined church crowning Glastonbury Tor is an interloper, for this dramatic hill was a sacred site long before it entered Christian legend.

❏ In the 1920s sculptress Katherine Maltwood, trying to fit the Arthurian quest for the Holy Grail onto British Ordnance Survey maps, found a pattern of Zodiacal figures in natural features (watercourses, roads and field boundaries) around Glastonbury.

❏ The mystery of Silbury Hill has inspired some splendidly silly theories – like the idea that it once boasted a giant pole on top to serve as the world's biggest sundial. Those who ascribed all prehistoric technology to visiting Egyptians (a fad which has been termed 'pyram-idiocy') managed to solve three puzzles of southern England at once: they decided a scientific expedition came from Ancient Egypt to England to build Stonehenge and Avebury, then erected Silbury Hill for the solemn burial of its leader.

❏ Two more huge (though lesser) mounds once stood near Silbury. The Marlborough Mound (above), first transformed by landscaping in the 18th century, then by later neglect, is now overgrown and crowned with a water tower; the Hatfield Barrow, or 'Giant of Marden', has disappeared entirely.

Giants on the Earth

Britain's most famous giants, the 70m (231ft) high 'Long Man of Wilmington', Sussex, and Dorset's 55m (180ft) 'Cerne Giant', are huge outline drawings cut into chalk hills. Most of Britain's c.50 chalk figures (from regimental badges to 'white horses') are modern – but the giants, although much restored, are not. They may depict Herakles (Hercules), a demigod with a popular cult in Roman Britain. Tales of giants exist worldwide. Mythmakers saw monuments like Stonehenge (the 'Giants' Dance') as giants' work and Stone Age burial chambers as 'giants' tombs'. Archaeologists still term massive Bronze Age masonry 'cyclopean' because ancient Greeks attributed it to the mythical giant Cyclops. Scientists hunted 'real giants' into modern times. In the 1930s they found fossil bones of an extinct giant – but it was a giant ape, *Gigantopithecus*. In 1931 they hailed giant footprints found in Mexico as 'definitely human'; later studies indicated a mammoth – or a U.S. Army camel. In the 16th century explorers reported living giants in Patagonia, South America, the leader 'so tall that our heads scarcely came up to his waist'. In 1831 naturalist Charles Darwin cut down the Patagonian giants: 'their height appears greater than it really is, from their large guanaco mantles, their long flowing hair, and general figure'. But some say Darwin missed the real giants, who hid – and still exist in hiding. In 1966 explorers found another giant tribe in South America. But the Krem-Akaore, 'a ferocious band of savages more than 7ft [2.1m] tall', shrank on closer examination to an average 1.8m (6ft) or less. Among ordinary mortals gigantism is usually due to medical disorders. This was the sad case of the world's tallest man, Robert Pershing Wadlow (1918-40) of Illinois. When his condition killed him, he was nearly 2.7m (9ft) tall – and still growing.

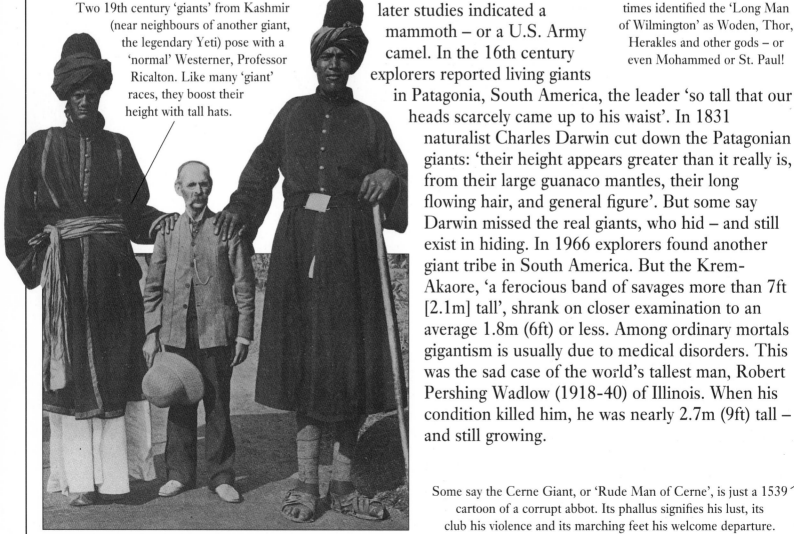

Antiquarians have at various times identified the 'Long Man of Wilmington' as Woden, Thor, Herakles and other gods – or even Mohammed or St. Paul!

Two 19th century 'giants' from Kashmir (near neighbours of another giant, the legendary Yeti) pose with a 'normal' Westerner, Professor Ricalton. Like many 'giant' races, they boost their height with tall hats.

Some say the Cerne Giant, or 'Rude Man of Cerne', is just a 1539 cartoon of a corrupt abbot. Its phallus signifies his lust, its club his violence and its marching feet his welcome departure.

The so-called Giant's Grave in Penrith, Cumbria, is an assembly of crosses and stones from several graves.

FACT FILE

❏ One of the best-loved giants of folklore was Little John, Robin Hood's sidekick. In 1784 Captain James Shuttleworth revealed an element of fact in the fiction when he dug up 'Little John's grave' (Derbyshire, England): a huge femur proved the grave's tenant well over normal height. Shuttleworth hung his trophy over his bed despite warnings that 'No good will come of it' – but after a run of bad luck he was persuaded to rebury it.

❏ Cutting white horses was such a popular custom in 18th century Britain that designers coined a name for it: leucippotomy. The only example from ancient times is the 'Uffington Horse' (above), which gave its name to Berkshire's Vale of the White Horse. Some think the dragon-like beast an Iron Age Celtic totem; others say it was cut by Saxon invader Hengist ('Horse') in c.450, or by King Alfred the Great in 871. It has even been 'identified' as a sketch of an ichthyosaur – a beast extinct c.65,000,000 years ago!

The hoodoo seas

In 1492 Columbus had compass trouble and saw strange lights in the sky as he sailed the Atlantic off Bermuda. Today the so-called 'Bermuda Triangle', some 647,000sq km (250,000sq mi) of ocean between Florida, Bermuda, and Puerto Rico, is said to have swallowed hundreds of ships and aircraft, leaving no wreckage or survivors. Earlier losses include U.S. Navy collier *Cyclops* with c.300 persons aboard in March 1918. The modern saga dates from the loss of 6 aircraft and 27 men on December 5, 1945. 'Flight 19', five Grumman Avenger torpedo bombers, flew from Fort Lauderdale, Fla. – and vanished, after a radio message: 'Everything is wrong . . . ocean doesn't look as it should'. A flyingboat sent to look for them vanished too. Many ships and aircraft have reported instruments going haywire and 'lights in the sky.' Triangle 'experts' speak of 'pockets of magnetic energy' that affect electronic gear – and attribute disappearances to 'warps in space-time', 'black holes', even alien kidnappers in giant U.F.O.s. But statistical analysis suggests the number of disappearances is about the average to be expected in waters where sudden, violent storms occur and strong currents swiftly disperse wreckage. In 1992 U.S. geologist Dr. Richard McIver theorized that undersea landslides release huge clouds of methane gas. Rising, the methane makes the sea 'boil', swamping ships, and interferes with navigational instruments, making planes wander off course and crash. Continuing undersea seismic activity buries the wrecks beyond all finding. One expert charts some 12 'hoodoo seas' worldwide. Among them are the 'Devil's Sea', centring on the Bonin and Mariana Islands in the Philippine Sea, south of Japan, and the 'Triangle of the Damned' in the Tyrrhenian Sea, between Sardinia, Sicily, and mainland Italy.

U.S. Navy supply ship *Cyclops*, steaming from Barbados to the American East Coast, had a radio – but sent no distress call before she disappeared in the 'Triangle' in 1918.

The map shows the generally accepted area of the 'Bermuda Triangle'. But some say the perilous zone runs from the Mexican Gulf to mid-Atlantic – the 'Devil's Triangle' – or even to the coast of Ireland.

UNITED STATES
BERMUDA
Miami
CUBA
HAITI
DOMINICAN REPUBLIC
JAMAICA
PUERTO RICO

Horseshoe Bay, Bermuda, looks a holidaymakers' paradise. But does some strange power, capable of snatching away ships and aircraft, lurk under or above these waters?

Tales of the 'Atlantic hoodoo' date from the 1800s – and inspired a sci-fi writer's 'non-gravitational vortex', sensationally illustrated in *Amazing Stories*, June 1930.

AMAZING STORIES

Scientifiction Stories by

A. Hyatt Verrill
John W. Campbell, Jr.
Edmond Hamilton

❑ In 1991 a deepsea exploration team of the Scientific Research Project, N.Y., claimed it had found the planes of Flight 19. A U.S. Navy spokesperson said that if they were the lost Avengers, they must remain undisturbed, as their crews' graves, and the Navy would seek a court ruling to that effect. Later reports suggest the wrecks were not those of Flight 19.

❑ Often repeated, but almost certainly untrue, is the tale of an Eastern Airlines flight in the Bermuda Triangle in the 1970s. The aircraft vanished from radar in Miami for 10 minutes, then reappeared and landed safely – with every timepiece aboard 10 minutes slow.

❑ Better authenticated is the story of Bruce Gernon, Jr., who flew a Beechcraft Bonanza plane from Andros Island, Bahamas, to Palm Beach, Fla., on December 4, 1970. Gernon flew into 'a glowing tunnel' of cloud, where instruments failed, his aircraft seemed to speed up and he and a passenger felt 'weightless'. On landing Gernon found his flight had taken 45 minutes instead of the usual 75; fuel consumption was down accordingly. Had he flown through a 'time warp'?

❑ Japan's 'Devil's Sea' is said to have swallowed up nine coastal freighters in 1950-54 – and then the survey ship *Kaiyo Maru No.5*, sent to search for their remains.

Lands beneath the oceans

Greek philosopher Plato (427-347 B.C.) told how 9,000 years before his time a great people ruled the island continent Atlantis until 'in a single day and night . . . Atlantis disappeared into the sea'. His account of an ideal state destroyed by the gods when it fell from grace – probably modelled on the Minoan culture of Crete, destroyed by a volcanic eruption c.1400 B.C. – was a moral fable, not history. But later scholars took it as fact that a drowned continent lay under the Atlantic Ocean. Advances in geographical and historical knowledge only added to the myth. With the discovery of America, Atlantis became a 'lost land bridge' between the New and Old Worlds. Later theorists located it all over the map, from Sweden to Africa, and peopled the ancient world with Atlantean refugees. In 1882 Ignatius Donnelly, ex-Governor of Minnesota, published his belief that Atlantis invented human civilization: *Atlantis, The Antediluvian World*. An instant bestseller, it inspired modern mythmakers' view of an Atlantean master race (perhaps colonists from space) with a supertechnology based on occult powers. The Atlantis craze also bred new 'lost continents'. Lemuria, in the Indian Ocean, began as a scientific hypothesis to explain animal distribution (notably of lemurs); Mu, in the Pacific, as a mistaken reading of Mayan script. Both quickly entered popular myth. Lemurians (Martians, Venusians, or hermaphrodite, telepathic, giant apes), and Muvians (the original, superior human race) joined Atlanteans as founders of human culture – and in 1926 writer James Churchward popularized Mu as the Biblical Garden of Eden, sunk by exploding gases 12,000 years ago. Today, New Agers perpetuate the legend; but geological surveys of the seabed convince most scientists that Atlantis, Lemuria and Mu existed only in human imagination.

Legendary priest-king Prester John was said to command a 'lost land' in the East – a kingdom of perfect peace and justice, free of poverty, sin and venomous plants or beasts.

Attempts to understand the restricted range of lemurs led to the idea of a lost continent: Lemuria.

Real lemurs are a far cry from the giant, preternaturally gifted Lemurians of fantasy.

U.S. politician and author Ignatius Donnelly (1831-1901) believed Atlantis saw the first highly advanced civilization, and dawn of all our arts and sciences.

This rather uninformative 19th-century map of Atlantis is based on the diagram published by Donnelly in 1882 – which he in turn based on the sketchy information provided by Plato.

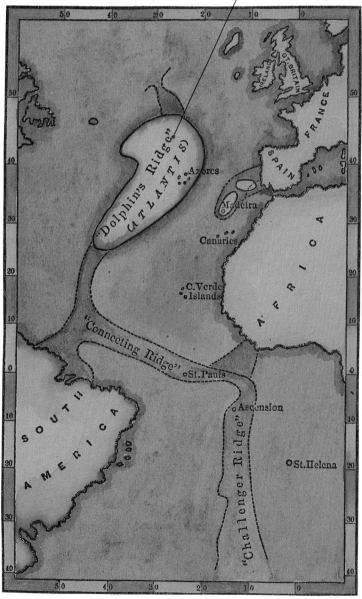

❏ Legend fills the seas of the world with lost lands. Factual coastal erosion inspired fictional drowned seaside kingdoms like England's fabled Lyonesse. When maps were made by hearsay and guesswork, travellers' tales spawned many mystery islands. As recently as 1969 a U.S. Navy destroyer logged a new example: a Caribbean island c.14m (45ft) across, bearing large palm trees, and sailing west at about 5kmh (3mph).

❏ English geologist Philip Lutley Sclater (in 1855 one of the 'inventors' of Lemuria) reckoned tales of lemmings diving into the sea and swimming towards the horizon proved lost continents had existed. Clearly, he said, the lemmings had a stubborn racial memory of Atlantis, and were trying to migrate there.

❏ Lemuria fanciers claim some Lemurians survived the loss of their continent by migrating to Atlantis – or possibly to the U.S.A. Some say they still inhabit caves near Mount Shasta, Cal. Dan Fry, who claims to have met Lemurians in 1950 in New Mexico, explains they have now moved to Mars, but still visit Earth (by U.F.O.) as sightseers. On the other hand, Hollow Earthers tell us Lemuria is not lost at all but remains inside the Earth, emitting harmful rays which cause our nightmares, wars, pestilences – and U.F.O. sightings.

Lure of the 'Money Pit'

In 1795 a hunter on tiny, uninhabited Oak Island, Mahone Bay, Nova Scotia, found traces of excavation and remains of block and tackle gear. Rumours of 'pirate gold' soon spread. By 1804 searchers had uncovered a 4m (13ft) wide shaft, sealed every 3m (10ft) by oak and clay platforms. At 27m (90ft) lay a 'cipher stone', said to mean '40ft [12m] below £2 million [then c.$12 million] are buried'. But at 33.5m (110ft) water flooded the shaft. At that depth, an 1849 expedition found, the 'Money Pit's' designers had dug a c.46m (150ft) tunnel to the shore, so that the change in air pressure when the shaft was excavated siphoned in the sea. In 1894 treasure seekers dynamited the flood tunnel, drilled to 53m (175ft), and found three links of a gold (or copper) chain. Then the sea poured in again: the explorers went bust trying to sink parallel shafts. In 1938 a U.S. engineer found a second flood tunnel at 46m (150ft). Undeterred by tragedy in 1965, when four men in the pit were killed by a pump's exhaust gases, a Canadian syndicate launched a $600,000 effort in 1967. A TV camera lowered to 65m (212ft) in the flooded shaft produced blurred images interpreted as a pickaxe, three 'treasure chests' – and a severed human hand. Today, after some 13 expeditions, the site is so torn up that even location of the original shaft is uncertain. If there is treasure in the 'Money Pit', who put it there? Popular belief says it is the hoard of pirate Captain William Kidd, hanged in 1701. A more likely theory is that in c.1780, in the Revolutionary War, when British H.Q. in New York was threatened with capture, Royal Engineers constructed the elaborate hide for the army's pay chests. There is no record of the British Army losing this treasure, suggesting that it was recovered when peace came in 1783 – and that the Money Pit has been empty ever since.

Villainous Captain William Kidd supervises the burial of his (suitably personalized!) treasure – perhaps on Oak Island – in this magazine illustration of 1902 by American artist Howard Pyle, famous for his stirring 'pirate pictures'.

❏ Before his execution Kidd valued his hidden treasure at the then enormous sum of £100,000 (at today's value, a multi-million dollar fortune). He vainly offered it to the British government in exchange for his life – then cursed all who went in search of it. Maps found in the 1920s among what were said to be Kidd's effects show an island much like Oak Island. Wilder theories link the Money Pit with fugitive Incas, Viking rovers, a crippled Spanish treasure ship – even with documents that may prove Francis Bacon wrote the plays of Shakespeare.

❏ In 1992 a U.S.-Australian syndicate invested some $160,000 in a hunt for a safe full of gold said to have been buried by outlaw Jesse James (above). According to his (self-styled) descendants Jesse James IV and his brother Woodson, the 'Jesse' gunned down in St. Joseph, Miss., in 1882 was an impostor. The real Jesse lived on as railroad and mining tycoon J. Frank Dalton of Granbury, Tex., dying in 1951 at the age of 107. He married 26 times – but still found time to bury his loot somewhere near Waco, Tex.

As an aerial photograph shows, a causeway now links the mainland with Oak Island – where the only riches gained have been by motels catering to tourists visiting the 'Money Pit' (right end of island).

The body of William Kidd, executed for piracy, hangs in chains to rot at London's 'Execution Dock', 1701. Kidd's ghost is said to walk on Long Island, N.Y., one of his lifetime 'haunts'.

Stately homes: stately ghosts

Holyrood Palace, where in 1556 Lord Darnley, husband of Mary, Queen of Scots, slew her reputed lover David Rizzio. Both are said to haunt the scene.

The 'stately homes of England' house stately ghosts. A much haunted site is the Tower of London, 'Death Row' for state prisoners for 800 years. The ghosts of the 'Princes in the Tower' (King Edward V and his brother, murdered there in 1483) lingered until their belated royal burial in 1674. More persistent phantoms include Sir Walter Raleigh, recalling 13 years' imprisonment as he paces the walls by moonlight; shrieking Guy Fawkes, tortured for his attempt to blow up Parliament; the Countess of Salisbury, re-enacting her grisly death in 1541 as the executioner chases her round the scaffold; and Anne Boleyn, second wife of much-married Henry VIII. In 1864 a Tower guard accused of sleeping on duty was cleared when witnesses backed his claim to have fainted when he met Anne's ghost. (The jobs of the famous 'Beefeaters' are not without peril: in 1800 the ghost of a huge black bear, presumably one 'baited' to death at the royal menagerie kept at the Tower in the 15th-17th centuries, is said to have caused a guard to die of fright.) Anne Boleyn must be the busiest royal ghost, riding a spectral barge upriver to the Tower, or revisiting her native Norfolk in a coach drawn by headless horses – her own severed head on her knee. She also visits Henry's palace of Hampton Court; so do his third wife Jane Seymour, prowling the Clock Court with a candle, and his fifth, Catherine Howard, still begging the king not to behead her (but he did). Hampton Court also boasts a nameless White Lady, and a Grey Lady who toils at a spinning wheel. St. James's Palace, London, has a macabre ghost: a blood-drenched man with cut throat. He is Sallis, valet to the wicked Duke of Cumberland, who is said to have murdered him in 1810, to keep him quiet, after seducing his daughter. The Duke was not brought to trial, but public outcry made him flee London.

At midnight, Windsor Park is haunted by the savage Herne the Hunter. Legend says he was a 14th century forester who hanged himself there, but the tale may have older roots in Celtic worship of a horned god.

A popular haunt, Hampton Court boasts a range of ghostly queens, ministers, royal servants and royal victims – from Cardinal Wolsey to Edward VI's old nurse.

Ghostly queen Jane Seymour is said to flit nightly up the stairway to her private apartments at Hampton Court.

❑ Glamis Castle, Scotland (below), family home of Queen Elizabeth the Queen Mother, has several ghosts – including a party of gamblers condemned to play until Doomsday a card game begun in the 15th century. No ghost, but a sinister legend, is the 'Monster of Glamis', said to be a hideously deformed, unnaturally long-lived son of the house, kept in a secret room. In 1865 a workman found the hideaway, emerged in a state of terror – and was packed off to Australia before he could tell his tale. Only the head of the family knows the true secret of 'the curse of Glamis', and traditionally passes it to his heir on his 21st birthday. But perhaps the 'Monster' will now remain a mystery forever: the 14th Earl (grandfather of Queen Elizabeth II) is said to have been so appalled that he refused to share the secret with his son.

Curse, jinx or hex?

Students of the occult make a distinction between a curse and a jinx. A curse is a weapon aimed at a particular person, as when an Aboriginal shaman 'points the bone' at a malefactor or a Voodoo sorcerer makes, then mars, a doll in the image of an enemy. A curse may work because the intended victim knows of it, believes in the curser's power, thinks he or she cannot resist – and simply loses the will to live. A jinx is less personal: it is when ill luck seems to attach to a particular artifact, typically a structure or ship that has seen accidental death in its building, or to an object, usually associated with violence of some kind, that brings tragedy to a succession of owners. A useful word for all phenomena of this kind is hex (German: *hexe*; 'witch'). The reader may decide whether the hexes examined here and on other pages are curses or jinxes. The 'Hope Diamond' is certainly jinxed. The 44.5 carat stone sold to Henry Hope in London in 1830 was probably the remnant of King Louis XVI's 'Blue Diamond of the Crown', a 67.1 carat gem which disappeared when that monarch lost his head in the French Revolution. Legend says it was mined in India in the 15th century, set in the forehead of a god's image – and stolen by a priest, its first victim. Some 20 owners have since suffered great misfortune. In the early 1900s a Russian prince decked his actress mistress with it, then shot her, then was assassinated. Sultan Abd-ul-Hamid II ('Abdul the Damned') of Turkey bought it for one of his wives in 1908, then tried to kill her, then lost his throne. U.S. press tycoon Edward Beale McLean bought it in 1911: he was ruined and died insane; tragedy plagued his family for 40 years. But the jeweller who bought the gem from McLean's heirs played safe: he gave it to Washington's Smithsonian Institute.

The Koh-i-Noor diamond now adorns the crown of England's Queen Elizabeth the Queen Mother. It is said to bring ill luck to male wearers.

Possession of the fabulous 'Hope Diamond' brought no joy to Turkey's Adb-ul-Hamid II ('Abdul the Damned', or the 'Great Assassin') (1842-1918).

The executioner holds aloft the severed head of King Louis XVI of France; January 21, 1793. The 'Hope Diamond' is said to have been cut from the unlucky monarch's huge 'Blue Diamond of the Crown'.

The 44.5 carat 'Hope Diamond' in its modern setting. It is said to have first adorned the forehead of an Eastern god – whose vengeance has struck down later owners.

Although it is said to have brought tragedy to her family, Mrs. Evelyn Walsh McLean seems calm as she wears the 'Hope Diamond' at a ball, 1941.

FACT FILE

❏ Another gem said to carry a jinx is the 106 carat Koh-i-Noor ('Mountain of Light') diamond. It belonged in the 18th-19th centuries to the Mogul emperors of India, whose realm crumbled; to a Shah of Persia who was assassinated; to an Afghan ruler who was deposed; and to Sikh princes whose domains, along with the great diamond itself, were taken over by the British. It is said to be unlucky only for men: Queen Victoria and other British queens have worn it without harm, but no male monarch has risked it.

❏ In the opera *Charles VI* by French composer Jacques Halévy (1799-1862) there is a 'cursing aria'. On the opera's opening night a stage hand dropped dead as the song was sung. In 1858 Emperor Napoleon III of France (above) ordered a 'command performance' – and narrowly escaped assassination on the same day. It is believed the unlucky opera has not been performed since.

Curse of the boy king

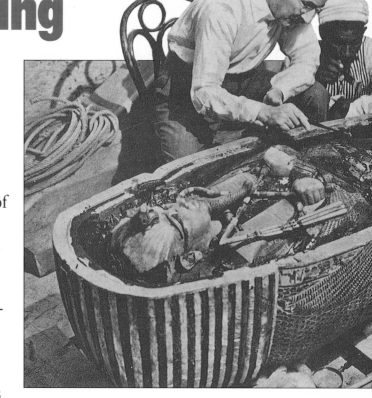

On November 26, 1922, Egyptologist Howard Carter broke a peace of c.3,000 years by opening the tomb of Egypt's boy king Tutankhamun (d.c.1340 B.C.). 'Can you see anything?' asked his backer, Lord Carnarvon. 'Wonderful things!' cried Carter, seeing treasures buried with the pharaoh's gold encased mummy. Some four months later Carnarvon (57) died in Cairo. As he raved of 'a bird . . . scratching my face', power failure plunged Cairo into darkness – and in England his pet dog howled and fell dead. So began tales of a curse. It was said that Carter found in the tomb the inscription: 'Death comes on swift wings to whoever disturbs the pharaoh's peace' – a reference to vulture goddess, Nekhbet. Her images were found with the mummy – and a great bird hovered above the tomb on the day of its despoilment. Sir Arthur Conan Doyle attributed Carnarvon's death to 'elementals [spirits] . . . created by Tutankhamun's priests to guard the mummy'. Within 7 years, only 2 of 13 Europeans present at the tomb's opening still lived; by the 1940s some 25 persons involved had died 'unnatural deaths'. Some theorized the pharaoh's priests had 'poisoned' the treasures; that unknown, deadly bacteria had remained effective for millennia in the sealed enviroment; even that ancient Egyptian scientists had impregnated the tomb with radio-active material. Howard Carter, who died in 1939 aged 66, opined 'sane people should dismiss such inventions with contempt'. In 1966 Cairo Museum's Director of Antiquities was reluctant to send Tutankhamun's treasures for exhibition in Paris. Leaving a meeting where his objections were overruled, he was killed in a traffic accident. His successor, Dr. Gamal ed-Din Mehrez, who dismissed all the deaths as 'coincidence', fell dead aged 52 in 1972, just as the boy king's gold mask left Cairo to go on show in London.

This golden figure of a falcon goddess was among Tutankhamun's magnificent grave goods. Also found were representations of the less pleasant vulture goddess, Nekhbet.

In 1924, nearly two years after breaking into the tomb, Howard Carter opened Tutankhamun's sarcophagus (stone outer coffin). Carter, chief 'guilty party' in disturbing the pharaoh, lived another 15 years.

As well as the sarcophagus for his mummy, the pharaoh's tomb contained several gold coffins like this, intended to hold various organs removed before mummification.

A golden fan with carved wood handle bears an embossed picture of the boy king, mounted in a chariot, drawing a bow to shoot down an ostrich whose feathers would line the fan's edges.

FACT FILE

❏ Most tombs (c.60) in the Valley of the Kings were probably looted not long after their building – suggesting the ancient Egyptians themselves cared little for curses. Tutankhamun's tomb remained virtually undisturbed because it was hidden by debris thrown up by robbers of the nearby tomb of Ramesses VI.

❏ Carter denied he found a 'curse' in Tutankhamun's tomb. Its only 'protection', he said, was a small lamp bearing the words: 'I prevent sand from choking the secret chamber.' Some say Carter destroyed the curse inscription to avoid scaring away his diggers; others believe he invented the curse to keep away sightseers and potential robbers.

❏ In September 1979 Tutankhamun's golden mask (above) was displayed in San Francisco. One of its guards, George LaBrash, suffered a stroke while on duty. In January 1982 he sued city authorities for having exposed him to the curse. His claim for compensation failed.

Doomed giants of the oceans

Although Captain Harrison commanded the 22,500-tonne *Great Eastern* – largest, fastest liner of her time – he was not happy. As the giant began trials in 1859, he learned of the death of her designer Isambard Kingdom Brunel; a burst steam pipe scalded to death six stokers; and his off-duty rest was 'rudely disturbed by constant hammering'. *Great Eastern*'s construction had bankrupted her builders and had seen several fatal accidents: one riveter simply 'disappeared' while working on her double hull. Her troubled career – with every unhappy incident, it is recorded, heralded by mysterious hammering from amidships – was never profitable, and in 1887 she was scrapped. In the hull, breaker's men found a skeleton clutching a hammer: the missing riveter, whose spirit had banged out warnings of disaster for nearly 30 years. Not long after, in 1898, U.S. novelist Morgan Robertson published *Futility*, tale of a 75,000 tonne, 'unsinkable' liner, *Titan*, sunk on an April night in the Atlantic after hitting an iceberg on her maiden voyage – with great loss of life because she carried only 24 life boats. On April 14-15, 1912, the 'unsinkable' *Titanic* (66,000 tonnes) went down in exactly the same way: of 2,224 persons aboard, 1,513 died – partly because she carried only 20 lifeboats. An unhappy giant of a later time was the German battle cruiser *Scharnhorst* (32,000 tonnes), launched in 1936 after an accident in building had killed 61 workmen and injured 110. In her first action in World War II gun turret accidents killed 21 men: many more unlucky incidents followed until, on December 26, 1943, she was sunk by British warships. Only 36 of her 1,900 crew survived: two, in a life raft, reached an Arctic shore, lit an emergency oil stove for warmth – and died when it exploded.

By far the largest ship of her time (1859-87), the 'accursed' *Great Eastern* is seen here in one of her few successful roles: laying the first undersea telegraph cable between Europe and North America in 1866.

Did her builders' boasts tempt fate? The 'unsinkable' *Titanic* steams out of Southampton on her maiden voyage, April 10, 1912.

Among those lost aboard *Titanic* was British journalist and Spiritualist William T. Stead (1849-1912). Like Morgan Robertson (but earlier, in 1882), Stead had published a story about a huge liner, ill equipped with life boats, sunk by an iceberg. Shortly before embarking on the fatal voyage, Stead revealed he had received 'spirit warnings' not to go.

It was alleged the *Titanic* was lost because her captain, eager to establish a record time across the Atlantic, steamed too fast in sea lanes strewn with icebergs.

Accursed cars and luckless locos

Some believe ancient artifacts like Egyptian mummies may carry a 'psychic charge', or be hexed. But surely not luxury automobiles – or diesel locomotives? On June 28, 1914, as Austrian Archduke Franz Ferdinand and his wife rode through Sarajevo, Bosnia, in a Graf und Stift touring car, Serbian terrorist Gavrilo Prinzip opened fire. The mortal wounding of the royal pair triggered off World War I. The car passed to Austrian General Potiorek, who went insane; then to another Austrian officer, who broke his neck when the car killed two pedestrians. A Yugoslav diplomat sold it after four accidents (one cost him his arm) to a doctor, killed when it overturned. Suicide and fatal accident claimed four more owners – the last with four passengers in a head-on smash. The accursed car survived, and was last reported in a Viennese museum. On September 23, 1955, when movie idol James Dean was introduced to famous British actor Sir Alec Guinness, he proudly displayed his new Porsche sports car. Guinness, a 'sensitive', warned: 'If you get in that car you will be dead by this time next week.' Days later 24-year-old Dean lay dead in the wrecked car. Towed away, it fell on a mechanic, breaking his legs. Its engine was fitted in a racing shell: its owner was killed in its first event. In the same race a driver using the Porsche's drive shaft in his rig also died. The original car was reassembled and put on display – until it literally fell to pieces (11 of them) for no apparent reason. A jinxed locomotive was British Rail's 100-tonne diesel *D326*, built in 1960. In 1962, hauling an express, it hit stationary passenger cars (18 dead; 33 injured). In August 1963, pulling a mail train, it was hijacked in the 'Great Train Robbery': its driver was badly hurt and the gang (later caught) snatched £2.6 million (c.$4.7 million). At last renumbering (*40126*) seemed to lift the curse.

Britain's jinxed locomotive, diesel *D326*, on the day of the 'Great Train Robbery', August 8, 1963. It was involved in further incidents until renumbering seemed to lift the 'curse'.

The wreck of the Porsche sports car in which actor James Dean died; September 30, 1955. The 'accursed' car survived to kill again.

Dean's role in *Rebel Without a Cause* (1955) seemed to foreshadow his death: he prepares to take part in a 'chicken run', an auto ordeal which ends in the death of a teenager.

The assassination of Archduke Franz Ferdinand and his wife in a 'hexed' automobile triggered a war in which many millions died.

❏ In 1991 Britain's Driver and Vehicle Licensing Agency announced the number '666' (according to the *Book of Revelations*, 'the number of the beast [Satan]') would no longer be used on the registration plates of British automobiles. 'People complained of funny things happening whenever they encountered a vehicle with this number,' said a spokesman for the government department, 'and there was so much hassle about accidents that we decided to scrap it.' Some churchmen welcomed the decision, but the Evangelical Alliance spoke of 'hysteria', pointing out that one of its own leaders was quite unworried by having '666' as a telephone number.

❏ In the late 1970s a British statistician made a detailed study of railway accidents, comparing the number of passengers on a train involved in a crash with the number of passengers on the same scheduled service on uneventful runs. He found that there were always significantly fewer passengers on 'unlucky' trains – giving rise to theories that many persons had been 'warned off' by unconscious premonitions of disaster.

❏ In July 1974 Neville Ebbin of Hamilton, Bermuda, aged 17, died after being knocked from his motorcycle by a cab. In July 1975 Neville's brother, 17, on the same cycle, died in collision with the same cab, same driver, on the same street.

Curse or coincidence?

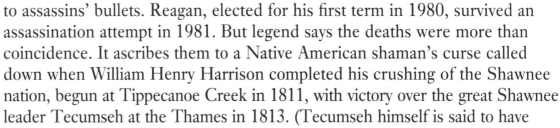

Legend says that when Shawnee leader Tecumseh was killed by William Henry Harrison's troops in 1813, a shaman put a curse on American presidents.

Moments after this picture was taken on March 30, 1981, President Reagan, first elected in 1980, supposedly an accursed year, was badly wounded by a would-be assassin.

Many Americans were relieved when President Reagan's second term ended in 1989. Not because they disliked him – but because he broke a 120-year chain of deadly coincidence. From 1840 onward every president elected in a year divisible by 20 had died in office. Three – William Henry Harrison (1773-1841), elected 1840; Warren Harding (1865-1923), elected 1920; Franklin Roosevelt (1882-1945), elected for third term 1940 – perished from natural causes. Four – Abraham Lincoln (1809-65), elected for first term 1860; James Garfield (1831-81), elected 1880; William McKinley (1897-1901), elected for second term 1900; John Kennedy (1917-63), elected 1960 – fell to assassins' bullets. Reagan, elected for his first term in 1980, survived an assassination attempt in 1981. But legend says the deaths were more than coincidence. It ascribes them to a Native American shaman's curse called down when William Henry Harrison completed his crushing of the Shawnee nation, begun at Tippecanoe Creek in 1811, with victory over the great Shawnee leader Tecumseh at the Thames in 1813. (Tecumseh himself is said to have been killed there by Richard Mentor Johnson, who ran as vice-president to Van Buren in 1836 on the regrettable slogan: 'Rumpsey, Dumpsey – Colonel Johnson killed Tecumseh.') But coincidences, events that are remarkably similar but appear to have no common cause, may be just as mysterious as curses. Biologist Paul Kammerer (1880-1926) proposed 'seriality', a theory that meaningful coincidences (which Jung in 1952 termed 'synchronicity') are far more common than we think, and may represent an as yet unknown law of the universe. Nobel Prize winning physicist Wolfgang Pauli (1900-58) pointed out that meaningful coincidences are a recognized principle in sub-atomic physics – a principle, he suggested, that may extend into the everyday world.

Gunman John W. Hinckley, Jr., lurks in a crowd of press men, part concealed by Police Officer Thomas K. Delahanty, one of the four persons he wounded.

President Lincoln (first elected in 1860) falls to an assassin's bullet: shot in the head by actor John Wilkes Booth.

President Franklin Roosevelt was elected for the third time in 1940. He died in his fourth term; April 12, 1945.

President Kennedy slumps into his wife's arms as a bullet shatters his skull; Dallas, Texas, November 22, 1963. Kennedy was the last victim of the supposed curse on presidents elected in a year divisible by 20. Some say Reagan's narrow escape 'broke' the curse.

Hexes and hoaxes

Hexes may 'work' not through supernatural power, but just because people believe they will. A case often quoted is that of a woman, apparently in perfect health, who died 'in panic' at City Hospital, Baltimore, Md., in 1969. She told doctors she was the only survivor of triplets born in 1946 (on a Friday 13th) in Okefenokee Swamp, Ga. The midwife, for reason unknown, told the mother the babies were hexed: the first would die before the age of 16 (killed in an auto accident, age 15); the second before she was 21 (shot dead, age 20); the third before she was 23. The patient died on the eve of her 23rd birthday: autopsy by specialists from Johns Hopkins University found no natural cause. But maybe hexes work because many people will believe anything – as editors of tabloid newspapers know. British tabloid *The Sun* showed how easy it is to manufacture a hex. One of Britain's favourite pieces of 'junk art' was a painting called 'The Crying Boy'. In September 1985 *The Sun* announced the picture was jinxed.

Homes where it hung had been destroyed or damaged by inexplicable fires – which left the painting itself untouched. Hundreds of readers wrote in to tell of disasters caused by the picture; thousands packed up their paintings and sent them to *The Sun* – which at Halloween organized a giant bonfire of the accursed art. It reported that some fire brigades asked to assist had declined because their personnel feared ill luck. In the U.S.A. in the 1970s-80s, reports of 'unlucky stones' resulted in a deluge of mail for staff at Volcanoes National Park, Hawaii, as tourists returned stones picked up on the slopes of the Mauna Loa volcano. Tabloids reported a Hawaiian legend that said such 'theft' angered volcano goddess Pele – and gave such a catalogue of death and destruction that people sent back their souvenirs at a rate of some 40 packages a day.

A witch's 'poppet' made in the image of a person it is desired to hurt is hanged by the neck and skewered with a rusty nail. The pain should be transferred to the victim.

Is this the wrath of the goddess Pele? One of several active volcanic craters (among them two of the world's largest) on Mauna Loa, Hawaii, erupts in smoke and flame, pouring out molten lava.

Stretching from Georgia into Florida, Okefenokee Swamp is about 1,810sq km (700sq mi) in area. Hexes are said to have struck down certain of its inhabitants.

An innocent seeming object – but this 18th century 'witch bottle' holds nails meant to transfix 'poppets' like that on the facing page.

❏ In 1978 the Chief Rabbi of Britain performed a solemn ceremony of purification at Clifford's Tower, York (below). The ancient fortification, it is said, had lain under a curse for nearly 800 years, since 150 Jews, falsely accused of ritual murder, committed suicide there to escape a Christian lynch mob on March 16, 1190.

❏ In the 1980s the council of King's Lynn was asked to move an 18th century obelisk endangered by vandalism. The councillors refused, noting it bore the words: 'Whoever moves this monument, let him die the last of his line.' The town's hooligans then smashed it – but apparently still live on.

❏ British tabloid newspapers in the late 1980s created the 'Tamworth Triangle': an accursed area of Britain's railway network, around Nottingham, where more than 100 fatal or serious accidents to people falling from trains had occurred within a few years. In 1991 an official investigation came up with a prosaic explanation: the doors on some of British Rail's passenger trains had faulty catches.

Lucky for some?

For vendors of lucky charms, superstitions mean good luck – and big business: Americans buy c.3,000,000 four-leaf clovers and c.10,000,000 rabbits' feet a year; Europeans c.1,000,000 and 5,000,000 respectively. Centuries of the Church's disapproval have had little impact on our desire to believe in charms and omens. People worldwide touch wood, wish on a star, nail horseshoes over doors, throw salt over their left shoulders, dread breaking mirrors and evade walking under ladders. Few remember the meanings of these actions. A 1960 survey showed 70 per cent of pedestrians would venture into traffic rather than walk under a ladder – but probably few knew that they were showing respect for the symbol of the Holy Trinity, the triangle between ladder and wall – or avoiding a reminder of an old-fashioned gallows. Touching wood 'for luck', we do not recall prehistoric worship of tree gods; and only dedicated folklorists see an image of the Mother Goddess's womb or Moon Goddess's horns in the lucky horseshoe. Fear of the number 13 is so widespread it merits a name: triskaidekaphobia. It has been linked with the 13 at Christ's Last Supper; the 13 guests at the fatal feast of Norse mythology when the god Balder died; the 13 members of a witches' coven. But it was 'unlucky' even before Christ's time – and not even those who fear it know why. Many folk still carry lucky charms, although the gruesome amulets of the past – dried toads; bits of hangman's rope – have given way to St. Christopher medals or four-leaf clovers (said to be the one plant Eve brought out of Eden). Faith in a charm may really 'bring luck' by inspiring positive thinking, and most such superstitions are harmless, or even helpful. Taken too far, however, they can dominate lives – and inspire evils like medieval witch-hunts.

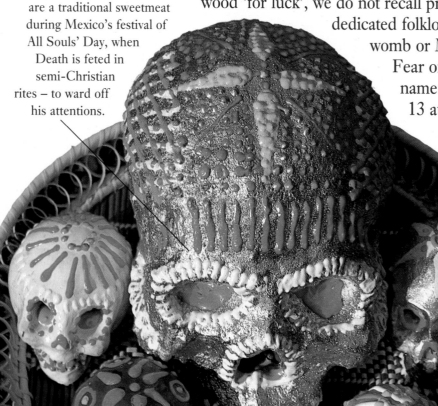

Gaily decorated sugar skulls are a traditional sweetmeat during Mexico's festival of All Souls' Day, when Death is feted in semi-Christian rites – to ward off his attentions.

Undertakers in ancient Egypt placed a carved scarab beetle, symbol of resurrection, over the heart of a mummified corpse as an amulet for the journey into the next life.

In the English Midlands, 'well dressing' – decking wells with pictures made of flowers – survives as an annual Church festival; but it began as a pagan rite to honour 'the gods below'.

'Lucky' horseshoes: made of the sacred metal iron and with a significant shape – to pagans, an image of the female parts (honouring the Mother Goddess); to Christians, a 'C' for Christ.

19   82

FOLLOW ME

Doomsday!

Thousands of followers of U.S. prophet William Miller (d.1849) gathered on New England hills on April 3, 1843 to face Doomsday. When the day ended and the world did not, Miller made updates extending to October 22, 1844. Millerites sold up, donned white robes (designed and profitably marketed by Miller himself) and headed for graveyards to meet the risen dead. One farmer bought robes for his cows, hoping to sell milk to thirsty travellers on the road to Heaven. Believing the dead would reach Heaven first, some tried to queue-jump by family murder and suicide. When the final Doomsday dawned without incident (except a 'Last Trump' panic caused by a farmboy tootling a cow horn) most of the c.100,000 Millerites gave up. Today other prophets warn that Earth is at risk: from nuclear power, 'greenhouse effect' – or, say more way-out soothsayers, comet strikes, space aliens' attacks or 'polar shift' (the Earth tilting to spill sea over land). Their slogan, 'The End is Nigh', is an ancient one. Many faiths have taught that God will end His creation in a cosmic battle between good and evil. This final conflict, Armageddon, will be preceded by war, earthquake, storm, famine and flood, and followed by Judgement Day for souls. In old times, natural disasters were held to confirm such fears. Aztec, Buddhist and Hindu teachers envisaged a cycle of creation and destruction, with each age worse than the one before, and the last (in which we now live) beyond redemption: the Hindu *kali yuga*, 'black age'. Although many modern cults say the Last Day is near, we may take comfort from the many mistaken prophets of Doomsday – but not from the Anglo-Israelite sect. Calculating a 1953 (originally 1936) Doomsday from pyramid measurements, they stuck to their guns when 1953 came and went: they said the world had ended – but unbelievers had failed to notice.

One of the Bible's most chilling images: the dawn of Armageddon, with the skeletal figure of Death, mounted on his pale horse, riding out to slay.

To some, Doomsday is part of a cycle – like the Flood of *Genesis*, which destroyed the world only to herald a new beginning in God's Covenant with Noah.

In Eastern religions the never-ending cycle of birth, death and rebirth – repeated creations and destructions – is symbolized by the ever-turning Wheel of God.

Doomsday: angels pour 'the vials of the wrath of God' on guilty Earth (*Revelations*. XVI).

❑ Armageddon (Hebrew: *har megiddo*, 'hill of Megiddo') takes its name from Megiddo in Palestine, where many major battles were fought in Biblical times because of its strategic position.

❑ Jehovah's Witnesses believe God set up His kingdom on Earth in 1914 to prepare for the end of the world. They teach that 'many now living will not see death', for Armageddon is due any moment now – or overdue, for the movement expected it in October 1975.

❑ In 1964, Jim Jones, paranoid leader of the People's Temple Church, announced the world would end in thermonuclear war on July 15, 1967. Despite his prediction's failure, his cult survived – until November 1973, when the world ended for Jones and 912 followers with mass suicide at Jonestown, Guyana.

❑ Christian faith in bodily resurrection of the dead at Doomsday was once very literal. People thought bodies would rise in the same condition they were buried in – so amputees had severed limbs buried with them, for fear of facing the Lord short of an arm or leg. This was the reason people so dreaded 'Resurrection men' (see later pages) who stole cadavers for surgeons to dissect – for how could bodily parts scattered among laboratories reunite on Doomsday?

The Devil's footprints

The Devil has left his mark on the map of Britain. Huge standing stones like the Devil's Arrows, Yorkshire, are known as rocks he hurled at churches; prehistoric tombs like the Devil's Den, Wiltshire, are his lairs. Legend says he dug the valley of the Devil's Dyke in a bid to drown Sussex churches, and built the Devil's Bridge over a Welsh river to trap the souls of those who crossed. Another Satanic visit, which left traces on the ground rather than the map, occurred in Devon in 1855. It was an unusually bitter winter. People froze to death, and suffered bread riots or starvation when snow cut off supplies. It seemed only natural the Devil should come to inspect his work – and on February 9 folk all over Devon awoke to find his footprints in the snow. For that was the only explanation that seemed to fit the tracks that ran everywhere, crossing locked yards, inacessible rooftops and high windowsills; even passing through walls. They were apparently left by a being that walked on two legs, with cloven hoofs – and, some say, claws. Several witnesses said they resembled donkey tracks – if a donkey could walk upright, fly on to roofs, squeeze through tiny gaps, and cover hundreds of miles in a single night. Convinced the Devil was abroad, country folk ran to consult the clergy or locked themselves indoors. Scientists tried to explain away the 'Devil's footprints', blaming beasts from kangaroos to badgers, toads, birds with iced-up feet – and human pranksters; later students of odd events added hopping mice, or marks caused by a rope trailed by a nocturnal balloonist! No one has explained why the tracks should dance across a county for just one night. And if, as one clergyman held, his parishioners' rotten morals inspired Satan's Devon holiday, must we believe no other district merited his attention?

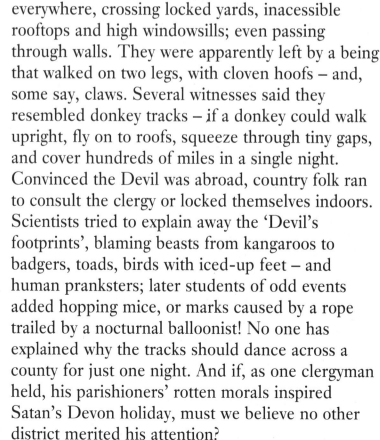

Local legend says these prehistoric monuments are the Devil's Arrows, with which the Arch-enemy sought (in vain) to smash a Yorkshire church.

The Devil's Bridge, Kirkby Lonsdale, Cumbria. The tale goes that the Devil built it in exchange for a promise of the soul of the first creature to cross it – but locals outwitted him by sending a dog over first.

This contemporary sketch of the 'Devil's Footprints' shows the clear resemblance, noted at the time, to the tracks of a donkey's shoe.

Naturalists can read the story of animal tracks in snow; but some remain undeciphered, like Yeti tracks in the Himalayas – and the 'Devil's footprints'.

Cloven hooves are the best known distinguishing mark of the Devil, dating back to Rabbinical tradition of the goat as an emblem of uncleanness (unholiness).

❏ Similar mystery footprints are occasionally reported elsewhere. To records from Scotland and France, English explorer Sir James Clark Ross added one from the Antarctic. In 1840 he visited uninhabited, icebound Kerguelen Island – and was amazed to see prints in the snow. They resembled a donkey's (on an island where certainly no donkey existed) but were single-track, as if it walked on two legs: just like the prints in Devon.

❏ If the 'Devil's footprints' were the work of a human agency, they may have been meant as more than a practical joke. At the time some clergymen were drawn to Puseyism, a neo-Catholic revival inspired by theologian Edward Pusey – to which traditionalists objected violently. This was the case in several of the parishes where the mystery tracks appeared – and led right up to church doors. At least one local newspaper saw the visitation as 'a warning to the Puseyites'.

❏ In the 1950s Scottish explorer James Alan Rennie saw in Scotland 'tracks every bit as mysterious as those seen in Devon'. But they were no mystery to him. He had seen similar tracks in Canada in 1924, when they actually formed before his eyes – made, he said, by 'some freakish current of warm air' condensing in the cold to deposit 'water-blobs' which left odd-shaped prints in the snow.

Into thin air

Folk once blamed disappearances 'into thin air' on lustful gods snatching up persons they fancied, or demons dragging off sinners to Hell. Now some blame mysterious abductions on U.F.O.s, or theorize that locations like the intersection of 'ley lines', said to join ancient sites, may form 'gateways' to another dimension. Ivan T. Sanderson mapped 10 'vile vortices' (one the Bermuda Triangle) where magnetic/climatic factors may create 'gravitational whirlpools' that whisk away objects or persons, who

American bandleader Glenn Miller, heading the American Band of the Allied Expeditionary Forces during World War II, was presumed killed in December 1944, when the plane in which he was flying from Britain to Paris disappeared. No wreckage or bodies were found. It was rumoured that the plane had been mistakenly shot down by an Allied fighter; and that Miller had survived the crash, but so dreadfully disfigured that he became a recluse.

sometimes return; sometimes not. Charles Fort called such removals 'teleportation'. A well attested case is that of a Spanish nun, Mary of Agreda, who in 1620 claimed she had made 'flights' to Mexico. Other nuns swore she had never left the convent. In 1622 Father Alonzo de Benavides, sent as a missionary to the Mexican Jumano people, reported they had already heard of Christ from 'a lady in blue'. A chalice she had given them was later identified as one from Mary's convent. Among famous disappearances are those of British diplomat Benjamin Bathurst, from a German inn yard in 1809; Rudolf Diesel, inventor of the diesel engine, from a North Sea steamer in 1913; and British politician Victor Grayson, who stepped into a train at Liverpool in 1920 and was never seen again. But Bathurst may have been abducted by Napoleonic agents; Diesel was in financial difficulties, and was suspected by Germany of selling industrial secrets to Britain; Grayson feared exposure of his bisexuality. More interesting is the case of U.S. author Ambrose Bierce. One of his stories (published 1878) created the legend (printed as fact as recently as the 1980s) of Tennessee farmer David Lang, who vanished in mid-stride in an open pasture but whose calls for help were heard long afterwards. In 1913, 70-year-old Bierce announced he was off to join Pancho Villa's rebels in Mexico – and vanished without trace.

Mexican bandit and revolutionary Pancho Villa (1878-1923) (left) with a henchman. Did U.S. writer Ambrose Bierce end his days among such tough customers?

Aviatrix Amelia Earhart and a co-pilot disappeared over the Pacific in 1937. Rumour says they had been asked to spy on Japanese-held islands.

Tales of mystery and horror made Ambrose Bierce (1842-?) famous. A noted cynic, nicknamed 'Bitter Bierce', he disappeared after running off to Mexico at the age of 70.

❑ Church authorities recognized Sister Mary of Agreda's '500 flights' to Mexico as genuine miracles. She was luckier than an unfortunate Portuguese merchant of Goa, India, who a few years after her flights, in 1655, was suddenly 'teleported' back to his homeland. The Holy Inquisition got word of his experience – and had him burned at the stake as a sorcerer.

❑ Rumours that Adolf Hitler (above) survived World War II and 'disappeared' to South America are certainly false – but stories that the body burned outside the *Führer*'s Berlin Bunker after his suicide on April 30, 1945, was not his may be true. In September 1992 Moscow's K.G.B. archives released movie footage said to show Hitler's unburned corpse. One Russian historian claims Hitler's body was secretly buried in the Soviet Union in 1945, dug up for re-identification in 1946, and finally destroyed in 1970.

From out of nowhere

Rarer than mysterious disappearances are people who appear 'from out of nowhere'. Some may be frauds, fleeing their pasts or seeking notoriety – like 'Princess Caraboo', who appeared in 1817 near Bristol, England, claiming to be a Javanese princess kidnapped by pirates. She was hailed 'the Wonder of the West', until her mother turned up to identify her as Mary Willcocks of Devon. But what of the two 'Green Children' found in Suffolk, England, in the 1100s? They spoke an unknown tongue and had green skins. Lodged with local landowner Sir Richard de Calne, the boy soon died; the girl lived to learn English and tell of her home in 'St. Martin's land'. She served Sir Richard for years; but he reported she was 'rather loose and wanton in her conduct'. A teenage boy found in Nuremberg, Germany in 1828 was also an enigma. He could write his name, Kaspar Hauser, but seemed ignorant of speech – or anything but sitting still, playing with toy horses, or eating bread and water. Within weeks he was able to tell of lifelong solitary confinement in a tiny, dark room. Was he the subject of a sinister experiment in sensory deprivation, or (as many thought) secret heir to some great house, deprived of his birthright and brought up in secrecy? In 1829 he died as strangely as he lived, stabbed – he said on his deathbed – by a masked man. Another enduring mystery was a woman rescued from drowning in a Berlin canal in 1920. She claimed to be Grand Duchess Anastasia, daughter of Tsar Nicholas II of Russia – reported killed with her family in 1918. The Tsar's surviving relatives could not agree whether she was or not, and for more than 50 years, under the name Anna Anderson, she was the centre of a legal battle that filled some 8,000 pages of court files. Eight years after her death, scholars still debate her case.

Folktales tell of 'alien' visitors like the Suffolk 'Green Children' straying into this world from a parallel, yet totally separate, world – a theme taken up by modern 'sci-fi' yarnspinners.

Kaspar Hauser appeared in 1828 in Nuremberg, unable to express himself but clutching a cryptic letter. The writer claimed to have kept him shut up for 16 years.

Tsar Nicholas II and his family in happier days. Today the skills of forensic scientists are turned to the task of identifying their presumed bones.

Did Grand Duchess Anastasia (seated far right with her family) die in 1918, as the official story has it, or did she escape, to reappear as Anna Anderson in Berlin?

Some mysterious appearances and disappearances may be cases of teleportation – an unlikely event which befell Victorian medium Mrs. Guppy.

❑ Russian officials announced in 1991 that bones found near Ekaterinburg, Urals, were certainly those of Tsar Nicholas II, Empress Alexandra and three of their children – but not of Anastasia or Tsarevich Alexis. Late in 1992 some of the remains were sent to Britain for D.N.A. ('genetic fingerprinting') tests. There was speculation that Prince Philip, husband of Britain's Queen Elizabeth II and near kin to Empress Alexandra, might be asked to donate tissue for comparison testing.

❑ Victorian medium Mrs. Guppy vanished from her London home one evening and materialized soon after, with a heavy thud, at a séance a few miles away. The arrival of 'the biggest woman in London' (104kg/230lb) made quite an impact, especially on one unfortunate who howled: 'Good God – there is something on my head!' The random nature of teleportation led Charles Fort (below) to describe it as a cosmic practical joke: the case of Mrs. Guppy certainly suggests a paranormal sense of humour.

What happened at Philadelphia?

W orld War II's strangest 'secret weapon' was tested, it is said, at the Philadelphia Navy Yard in October 1943. It was the U.S. Office of Naval Research's 'Project Rainbow', an attempt to make a ship invisible by 'electronic camouflage'. Albert Einstein was personally involved in this practical application of his theories suggesting that space and time are not absolutes. An 'electromagnetic force field' c.90m (300ft) across was created round the 1,240 tonne destroyer escort U.S.S. *Eldridge*. A green mist enshrouded the ship; then, in a 'space-time warp', it vanished – 'teleported' to the harbour at Norfolk, Va., some 480km (300mi) away. Minutes later the *Eldridge* reappeared at Philadelphia, apparently unharmed. But effects on her crew proved deadly. Some died; some went insane; some were mutilated by spontaneous combustion (see earlier pages); some underwent periods of 'transparency' during which they could walk through solid objects. The Navy confined survivors in top security hospitals. The story was not told until 1956, when Ufologist Morris Jessup made public information said to come from a merchant seaman who had been an eyewitness (although it seems unlikely a 'top secret' experiment would have been made in view of all comers). The U.S. Navy has always denied the 'Philadelphia Experiment' took place – but some allege a cover up, seeing sinister implications in Jessup's suicide in 1959 and claiming surviving witnesses are still silenced by threats from government agencies. What really happened? The story may stem from garbled accounts of research into 'radar invisibility' during World War II, when the German Navy once announced it had developed a 'magic paint' that made U-boats immune to electronic detection. It had not, but certainly research in this field was made by both Allies and Axis.

Surrendered U-boats, 1945. Late in World War II – as a cover-up for new 'snorkel' gear that made submarines more elusive – the German Navy claimed to have developed a 'magic anti-radar paint'.

A nuclear submarine under repair at Norfolk, Va., long a major U.S. naval base – and the reported scene, in 1943, of the brief 'materialization' of a 'time warped' warship.

□ U.S.S. *Eldridge* was apparently none the worse. She survived World War II and was sold in 1951 to the Greek Navy, serving as the frigate *Panthir* into the 1980s.

□ The U.S. Navy likely never practised 'magic', but some top commanders of World War II were noted mystics. Air Chief Marshal Dowding, who led the R.A.F. to victory in the 'Battle of Britain', was a Spiritualist, and in 1943 published a book, *Many Mansions*, containing 'spirit messages' from dead flyers. America's General George S. Patton (above) was a believer in reincarnation, claiming to have been a 'warrior woman' in one former life. Admiral Takijiro Onishi came near dismissal from the Imperial Japanese Navy: first for suggesting naval aviators should be selected by graphology (analysis of character from handwriting); then for allocating milliards of yen to fund a charlatan who claimed to able to change water to petrol. Onishi survived to help plan the Pearl Harbor attack and, later, to found the *kamikaze* suicide aircraft squadrons.

Modern 'magic camouflage': state-of-the-art low observables technology and an ultra-streamlined body make the U.S. Air Force's F-117A 'stealth fighter' near invisible to enemy radar.

The theories on time and space of Albert Einstein led some to consider the viability of 'invisibility' or even 'time travel'.

Invasion of the bodysnatchers

From early times cadavers were stolen from tombs for 'medical magic'. Physicians prescribed 'mummy' (parts of corpses) for many ailments: leg bones ground up in wine for rheumatism, powdered skull for epilepsy. In 1300 the Church ruled that desecration of the mortal body harmed the immortal soul, and forbade dissection of 'images of God'. For centuries this held back medicine: Andreas Vesalius (1514-64), pioneer anatomist, was condemned to death by the Inquisition for 'bodysnatching'. By the late 18th century most civilized nations had relaxed anti-dissection laws (including most states of the U.S.A., although New York Hospital was wrecked by an anti-dissection mob in 1788). But in Britain only the bodies of certain criminals (doomed to dissection after execution as 'a peculiar Mark of Infamy') went to anatomists. Corpses (shipped as salt fish) were imported

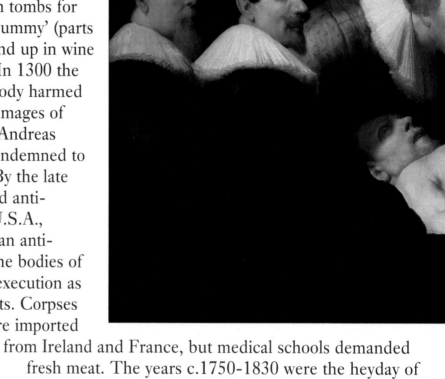

Pioneer anatomist Vesalius was condemned to death for 'body snatching'. The sentence was commuted to a pilgrimage – on which he died.

from Ireland and France, but medical schools demanded fresh meat. The years c.1750-1830 were the heyday of bodysnatchers: 'Resurrectionists', 'Grips', or 'Sack-em-up men'. The latter name came because bodies were taken naked from their graves: British law said stealing a body was only a misdemeanour, but stealing grave clothes or coffins a felony. One 'Grip' caught with 30 corpses (including a tub of pickled babies) got a small fine for bodysnatching, but 7 years' jail for stealing a shroud. The trade was profitable – surgeons paid up to £12 (then c.$70) each for prime subjects – and it is estimated that more than 1,000 Britons a year were 'resurrected' in c.1800-30. Two Edinburgh 'Grips' spoiled it. Too idle to dig, William Burke and William Hare murdered some 16 guests at their squalid lodging house in 1826-28 and sold the still warm bodies to a local surgeon. The scandal of their trial was largely responsible for the Anatomy Act of 1832, which made c.600 corpses a year legally available for research.

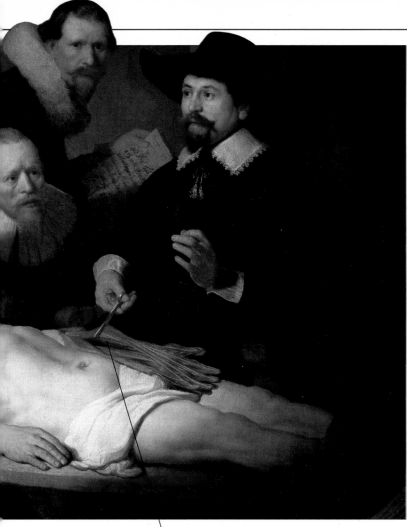

Bodysnatcher William Burke was hanged for murder (and then anatomized); January 1829.

Hare escaped the gallows by ratting on his partner – dying, it is said, a blind beggar.

The corpse shown in Rembrandt's magnificent *Anatomy [Lesson] of Dr. Nicolaes Tulp* is said to be that of Adriaan Adriaansz, a 28-year-old criminal from Leiden, hanged in 1632.

'Mort safes' like these – heavy iron cages to be placed over a new grave – were developed in Scotland to keep out the 'Grips' in the 18th-19th centuries. They were rented out by the week to cautious mourners.

Dicing with death

'Human salamanders' have been around since the *Old Testament* told how Daniel survived the Babylonian fiery furnace, and immunity from fire has long been seen as a mark of religious grace. In medieval 'trial by ordeal' an accused who could carry a red-hot ploughshare three (or seven) paces without hurt (or with burns that healed within three days) was judged innocent. It is said to be easy to walk swiftly across burning wood or ash, making only brief contact with a material of low thermal conductivity, but some firewalkers, notably Buddhist and Hindu holy persons, walk slowly over stones heated to c.430°C.(800°F.) – and sceptical witnesses have testified their feet are not treated with protective substances. Most think firewalking is a matter of faith (a kind of self-hypnosis) or, in the case of Westerners who perform the feat, nerve: stride out briskly and all is well – he who hesitates gets burned. Scientific tests are said to show that some who withstand painful rituals are able to slow down their brain waves to the 'theta frequencies' of sleep. At Kataragama, Sri Lanka, firewalking is part of annual Hindu religious ceremonies that include ritual mutilation. In religious ecstasy, devotees slash themselves with knives and thrust steel skewers through their tongues and cheeks. Some submit to having as many as 50 hooks embedded in their backs: with cords tied to these, some swing from frames, others pull loads of offerings to the temple. None shows pain; the wounds do not bleed. Young Westerners have now adapted a ritual of the Pentecost islanders of the South Pacific, who prove their manliness by jumping from 27m (90ft) bamboo towers with fibre ropes tied to their ankles to arrest the fall. A Western 'bungee jumper', in lycra suit and body harness, freefalls from c.60m (200ft) or more, then bounces like a yo-yo at the end of a latex rope.

A Hindu holy man stands on sharp sword blades during ceremonies at Kuala Lumpur, Malaysia. The devotees of many faiths practice mortification of the flesh as a sign of humility before their gods.

Although a fair number of Westerners have performed the feat, firewalking as a religious rite is mainly an Eastern practice. Here, worshippers in Hong Kong tread hot embers in a Chinese festival in honour of the Great Monkey God.

A needle transfixes the cheek of a Javanese dancer. Laboratory experiments suggest that religious ecstasy helps such persons block out pain with 'theta waves' from the brain.

Like their feet and bodies, the light silk or cotton clothing typically worn by firewalkers is unharmed.

A 'sidewalk showman' in Calcutta uses advanced yoga techniques, giving great control over breathing and other bodily functions, to perform a remarkable feat.

❏ On May 21 every year, to mark the miraculous rescue of saints' images from a burning church in c.1250, villagers at Lankadas, north Greece, dance for up to 30 minutes in a fire pit c.3.6m (12ft) square. Scientists who studied the ceremony in 1980 measured the temperature of the coals at 500°C. (932°F.), while thermocouples fitted to the dancer's feet registered only 180°C. (356°F.). 'Faith is needed', said a dancer in 1982 – after a British witness who attempted to join in was rushed to hospital with third-degree burns.

❏ One of the U.S.A.'s most famous 'human salamanders' was, appropriately, a blacksmith: Nathan Coker of Easton, Md. In 1871 it was reported that he could stand with bare feet on a white-hot shovel until it cooled, juggle pieces of metal taken from his fiery furnace and gargle with molten lead.

❏ Feats of tower divers, bungee jumpers and 'base jumpers' (who make parachute jumps from high structures) are overshadowed by the involuntary achievement of Nicholas Alkemade, a Royal Air Force sergeant of World War II. On March 24, 1944, Alkemade jumped from a flaming Lancaster bomber over Berlin without a parachute and fell c.5,490m (18,000ft). Young trees, thick undergrowth and deep snow broke his fall, and he had only minor injuries.

Food for thought!

'Milwaukee Monster' Jeffrey Dahmer stands trial in 1991. He confessed to 11 murders, and to having cooked and eaten parts of his victims.

In the 1970s 'anthropologist' Oscar Kiss Maerth claimed that early humans developed intelligence through a diet of brains. The cleverest 'ape people' trapped and butchered less able contemporaries, and ingested their abilities along with the contents of their skulls. (Maerth suggested that women, less physically capable of murder, were thus historically doomed to be less intelligent than men!) We may laugh at such theories, but if a spate of 'cannibal killings' in the 1980s-90s – like the case of 'Milwaukee Monster' Jeffrey L. Dahmer, alleged in 1991 to have slaughtered and part eaten several young men – is a guide, there are still people who hold the very ancient belief that human qualities can be 'stolen' by eating the flesh and/or drinking the blood of their possessors. Cannibalism has been far more often practised for magical purposes than out of a taste for human flesh. Most persons who have eaten fellow humans for non-magical reasons have done so simply to survive. Even instances of ritual cannibalism may have been much exaggerated. Spanish conquerors claimed that the Aztecs and other South American peoples ate sacrificial humans. Those who unquestioningly accept this should remember that early opponents of Christianity made the same charge, pointing out that at their 'love feasts' Christians ate the 'body and blood' of Christ. Eating people is not only wrong – it may also endanger your health. Some tribal peoples of New Guinea consume the brains of a recently deceased (in former times, ritually slaughtered) relative at the 'name feast' of an infant, who then takes that relative's name. It is now known that this practice spreads *kuru* ('shivers'), a fatal degenerative disease of the central nervous system caused by a virus like that responsible for 'Mad Cow Disease', a recent Western health scare.

A tribeswoman in New Guinea displays a mutilated hand. She is said to have cut off her fingers and burned them as part of a religious ceremony.

Caged like a wild beast, Russian 'cannibal killer' Andrei Chikatilo is tried in 1992 for an estimated 55 murders.

Cannibals prepare to feast: an old engraving of a type once popular among people who liked to think themselves superior to 'savage' (i.e., coloured) races.

FACT FILE

❏ America's most famous case of 'necessary cannibalism' was probably that of the 'Donner Party'. Snowed up in the Sierra Nevada in winter 1846, some members of George Donner's California-bound wagon train ate each other in order to survive. One man from the party was later tried for murder (he admitted to eating five persons), acquitted – and cashed in on his notoriety by opening a restaurant in San Francisco. He was luckier than a snow-bound trapper who is said to have been convicted of murder and cannibalism later in the century by a politically biased judge, who opined: 'Maybe you had to do it to survive. But there were only five Democrats in this county – and you ate three of them!'

❏ Male chauvinists like to point out that women's brains are smaller than men's. They are – a male brain averages around 1,424g (50.3oz) in weight; a female brain around 1,265g (44.7oz) – but scientists say that brain size, within normal parameters, has little to do with intelligence. An autopsy on Nobel Prize winning novelist Anatole France (1844-1924) (above) revealed that his brain was only about half average weight.

Hit or myth?

Most of us have heard an 'urban legend'; typically, an amazing experience of 'a friend of a friend of mine'. Tales of venomous spiders that crawl from store bought pot plants (usually yuccas) and 'alligators in the sewers' are exaggerations of real incidents – nasty insects are found in exotic plants and fruit; *The New York Times*, February 10, 1935, reported a 2.1m (7ft) alligator in a sewer on East 123rd Street, possibly dropped from a ship on the East River – but we must hope the micro-waved cat (or baby!) is fictitious. Students of modern folklore say the new legends differ little from ancient ones. Medieval folk who said King Arthur 'slept' to re-emerge in time of need have much in common with moderns who like to believe Elvis Presley is alive (maybe as a fast food cook in Nowhere, Minn.). Many urban legends are international – but one recorded in 1991 is specific to southern France, where forest fires then raged. The body of a scuba diver, it is said, was found in a burned out area: he had been siphoned up by firefighting planes swooping on the ocean to fill their water tanks. A British classic is the myth of 'Springheeled Jack', a demonic figure who terrorized London in 1837-38 and made sporadic reappearances until as late as 1904. His mighty leaps were attributed to springs in his boot heels – but some said he was an insane circus acrobat, vowed to frighten 30 persons to death, or even a trained (cleverly disguised!) kangaroo. A modern classic is the 'vanishing hitch-hiker', maybe dating from Chicago's 'Resurrection Mary' of the 1940s. 'Mary' hitches a ride with a young man, agrees to date him, and gives her address. He later goes to her home and is told she died years ago – killed near the spot where he picked her up – and has been trying to get home, on the anniversary of her death, ever since.

Myth says the sewers of American cities (some far from the Mississippi, where this specimen lives) are infested by alligators – perhaps originally dumped there as unwanted pets.

Corporal Dawie van Jaarsveld gave a ride on his motorcycle to a female 'phantom hitch-hiker' near Uniondale, South Africa, in April 1978.

One of Victorian England's favourite myths was that of 'Springheeled Jack'. He was not always shown as a villain: here he scares away bodysnatchers from their prey.

Tabloid newspapers' frequent 'sightings' of Elvis Aaron Presley (seen here in a 1973 photograph) are eagerly accepted by some fans unwilling to accept the fact of 'The King's' death in 1977.

❑ The outrages (he specialized in sexual harassment of girls) of 'Springheeled Jack' were probably the work of a succession of unpleasant practical jokers. The original in 1837-38 may have been Henry de la Poer Beresford, Marquis of Waterford (1810-59), a notorious and ruthless gagster. Beresford had protuberant eyes – 'Jack's' victims often described him as bug-eyed – and, newpapers of the time alleged, could often be located at or near the scenes of 'Jack's' attacks.

❑ A grim tale that seems tailormade for today tells of a man or woman who has a one night stand with a stranger. He or she wakes to find the partner gone, leaving a note: 'Welcome to the A.I.D.S. club.' But Dr. Paul Smith, Professor of Folklore, Memorial University, Newfoundland, traces this myth back to the Middle Ages – when the message read: 'Welcome the Black Death!'

❑ A cautionary fable certainly for our time is that of a youngster who accepts a drink (or drugs) from a stranger. The victim wakes up hours later with a surgical scar on his or her back. Medical examination reveals a kidney is missing – 'hijacked' by an unscrupulous surgeon for sale in the Middle East. Police in Southampton, England, claimed to have been told of some 50 such cases in 1992: all concerning 'a friend of a friend'; none genuine.

SUPERFACTS

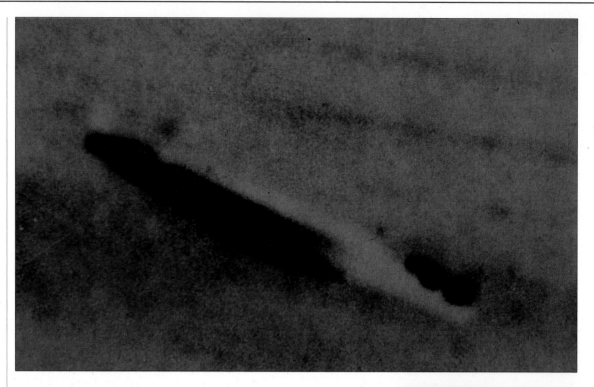

▲ Beware of hoaxes!

Enthusiastic Ufologists claim medieval chronicles contain many mentions of 'strange sky craft', or U.F.O.s (above). A famous account, still printed as fact in some books, is said to have been compiled at Ampleforth Abbey, England, in 1290. The monks witnessed 'a large round silver thing like a disc, that flew slowly over them and excited the greatest terror. Whereat Abbot Henry cried that it was the fault of Brother Wilfred, an adulterer . . . ' Unfortunately this picturesque account, in Latin, was concocted by two British schoolboys, who managed to get it published in *The Times* newspaper in 1953.

Saved by logic

Today we may ascribe 'paranormal travel' to U.F.O. kidnapping or teleportation: earlier folk blamed the Devil. In the 9th century four travellers arrived at Lyons, France, in 'a cloud-ship'. They said they had been hijacked by men with strange powers, including air transport. The locals thought it sounded fishy and decided to stone them to death. But local Archbishop, St. Agobard, turned his logic on the case. Cloud-ships, he said, did not exist – so the strangers must be innocent of the crime of riding in one. They were released.

U.F.O.-gate?

One of the first men to claim to have been taken for a ride in a U.F.O., in 1949, was Daniel Fry, then an engineer at White Sands missile range, N.Mex. In 1968, claims Fry, he acted as an intermediary between an E.T. called 'Alan' and President-elect Richard Nixon, passing on 'Alan's' advice as to whom the President should employ on his White House staff.

Smoke without fire

Popular accounts of spontaneous human combustion still cite the 'triple finger of fire' that struck down three unconnected individuals on April 7, 1938. In

Cheshire, Britain, George Turner burned to ashes in his lorry – a can of petrol beside him was untouched; in Holland, Willem ten Bruik burned up at the wheel of his Volkswagen; at sea, John Greeley went up in flame at the helm of the *Ulrich*. It was an impressive coincidence – until sceptical researchers checked up. There was no record of a ship named *Ulrich*, or of the death of

George Turner – and Willem ten Bruik's Volkswagen is equally fictitious: Volkswagen production did not begin until May 1938.

▼ God's broad acres

By the early 19th century Britain's city churchyards were so crowded that cadavers often were buried only a few inches deep: an easy mark for bodysnatchers as well as a danger to public health. A similar problem in some American cities was solved by Dr. Jacob Bigelow of Boston, who pioneered 'garden cemeteries' (below) in the countryside. The first was Mount Auburn Cemetery, Cambridge, Mass., a former picnic ground for Harvard students, opened in 1831.

Batman scam

As late as the 17th century, unscrupulous surgeons profited from an 'exorcism' scam. They diagnosed 'demonic possession', curable by a simple operation. As the quack made a small incision in the patient's abdomen, his assistant released a live bat from a bag – and the relieved patient was told to watch the liberated 'demon' fly away.

Man for the job

A few months before the end of the Pacific War in 1945, Lieutenant Hiroo Onoda of the Imperial Japanese Army was given command of a guerrilla force on Lubang Island, Philippines, and ordered to fight 'until we return for you'. Onoda's war lasted 30 years: he waged a campaign in which all his men died (and some 30 Filipinos were killed) until March 1974, when his former C.O. was sent back to Lubang to order him to surrender. In June 1992 the Japanese government funded a 'survival skills' school for teenagers in the Fukushima mountains. Its director was a man uniquely qualified for the task: Hiroo Onoda.

Dirty tricks

In 1953 the American illusionist John Mulholland was asked to write a 'top secret' manual on conjuring tricks. It was intended for the use of C.I.A. agents, who might need to drug drinks, switch documents, or perform other sleight of hand feats during their missions.

▼ Stone magic

Despite protests by clergy, British locals held to the belief (as some still do) that ancient stone circles had powers of healing and fertility. Parents carried sick children to the stones as a cure; barren women rubbed themselves against rocks with nicknames like 'the Stone Mare' in the belief they would fall pregnant. Lusty fertility rites persisted at circles like Avebury Rings (below) into the 18th century: a shocked 16th century antiquarian recorded that 'of fortie, three-score or a hundred maidens going there overnight, there have been scarcely the third part returned home undefiled'.

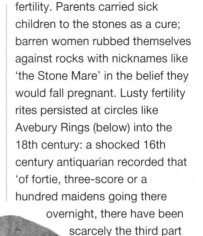

SUPERFACTS

Cannonball caper ▶

A favourite experiment of Flat Earthists, who also claimed Earth stood still in space, was to fire a cannon vertically into the air. The ball fell back to Earth at its launching point – thus proving Earth was stationary. Opponents of the astronomer Galileo (1564-1642) (right) used this trick to refute his claim that Earth revolved, scoffing at his explanation that the cannonball itself turned with the turning Earth. The Inquisition ordered Galileo to keep silent or face heresy charges. As late as the 1920s, 200 years after Newton's 'law of gravity', Britain's Zetetics tried to confound opponents with the cannonball caper.

▼ Genesis in Atlantis

In the 1920s Karl Zschaetzch (who himself sounds like a lost race!) combined legendary lost continent Atlantis (below) and the Biblical Creation story. His Atlantis was an earthly paradise whose people lived in perfect, vegetarian innocence until a woman (Eve) brought them the demon alcohol in the form of cider (i.e. apples – *The Bible*'s forbidden fruit). The corrupted Atlanteans were 'expelled from Eden' when a comet strike destroyed their home – but a few survivors married into inferior races of other lands to found the modern human race.

Auto-hex

Hexing is an ancient art of African shamans – but some keep their maledictions well up to date. It is reported that a favourite curse against males in modern Ghana is: 'May your sexual organ become as bent as the gearshift of a Mercedes Benz.'

◄ Triskaidekaphobics

For the same reason that British Airways' Concorde (left) has no Row 13, many hotels in the U.S.A. and Europe have no floor or rooms with the 'unlucky' number. The London Hilton, however, has a floor 13 – and reported in 1992 that its room number 1313 is much in demand. At London's famous Savoy Hotel a carved black cat, Kaspar, is always given a place setting at any meal where there are 13 diners. The custom dates from 1898, when South African millionaire Woolf Joel gave a dinner for 13 persons – ignoring the warnings of triskaidekaphobic friends – and was murdered soon afterwards.

Kingdoms under the sea

Britain claims three legendary drowned kingdoms: Tyno Helig and the Lowland Hundred, off Wales, and Lyonesse, off Cornwall. Tradition says the gods drowned Tyno Helig to punish its ruler's sins; the Lowland Hundred was swamped when a drunken partygoer opened its sluice gates; Lyonesse fell to the sea's wrath. The areas where all three are said to lie were indeed inhabited in ancient times, but the great kingdoms are fiction, perhaps inspired by 'drowned palaces' – really natural rock formations – visible at low tide.

The long sleep

Some researchers believe everyone has 'extra-sensory perception' (E.S.P.) potential, but few have conscious access to it. It may be released in 'Out of Body Experiences', reported by persons who 'die' and then revive, or in subjects under hypnosis – and has appeared in coma victims. One was Molly Fancher of Brooklyn, who lay in a coma for 46 years, from 1866. In 1875 doctors found the unconscious woman could describe the contents of sealed documents and say what persons were doing many miles away. In 1912 she revived – and her gift vanished. She died in 1915, aged 73.

Waters of forgetfulness

It has been claimed that a disaster zone of Bermuda Triangle type lies along the U.S.A.-Canada border in the area of the Great Lakes, roughly between 76-92°W. and 41-49°N. Since the 19th century, it is said, many ships and, later, aircraft, have inexplicably disappeared there. Unlike its more famous counterpart, the 'Great Lakes Triangle' sometimes gives up survivors of the mysterious wrecks – but they can never remember in what ways their craft were lost.

Royal understatements

King Louis XVI of France ties with England's George III as history's most incompetent diarist. Louis's entry for July 14, 1789, when the storming of the Bastille prison by Parisians marked the beginning of the revolution that was to cost him his head, was: 'Nothing happened.' George's entry, 'Nothing of importance happened today', was made on July 4, 1776. (It would, of course, be weeks before a ship brought the latest news from his American colonies.)

▼ Unlikely tale

An outrageous hoax perpetrated by Britain's *Sunday Sport* tabloid was its 1988 story: 'World War II bomber found on Moon.' It was followed by 'World War II bomber found on Moon vanishes'; and finally by 'World War II bomber back from Moon', describing how the U.S. Privateer aircraft, 'catapulted to the Moon by a Black Hole above the Bermuda Triangle' (below) had been landed at London's Heathrow airport by a pilot who had been in suspended animation since 1944.

SUPERFACTS

▼ Hot foot

Dr. Jearl Walker, Professor of Physics at Cleveland State University, Ohio, theorized that fire walkers (below) were able to perform unharmed not through faith alone, but because sweat or water on their feet made a protective layer because of the 'Leidenfrost effect' (named for a German scientist who, in 1756, observed that water dropped on a very hot surface 'dances', taking longer to evaporate than on a cooler surface). In 1980 Dr. Walker tested his belief in a home-made, 1.5m (5ft) fire pit: sometimes it worked – but sometimes, to his sorrow, it did not.

Devil's 'deuce'

American gamblers say it is bad luck to receive a $2 dollar bill ('deuce') when playing, perhaps because 'deuce' is another word for the Devil. To avert the curse, a corner must be torn from the bill; if it already lacks all its corners, it must be destroyed.

Accursed castle ▶

Archduke Franz Ferdinand, killed in a 'jinxed car' in 1914 (see earlier pages), is said to have courted doom by living in 'accursed' Miramar Castle (right), near Trieste, Italy. The picturesque Habsburg palace was built in 1856 for Archduke Maximilian: his reign as Emperor of Mexico ended in front of a firing squad; his wife went insane. Empress Elizabeth and her son Archduke Rudolf lived there in the 1880s: Elizabeth was assassinated; Rudolf committed suicide. In World War II it was taken over by the British Army, which lost two generals there to sudden, unexpected heart attacks.

By Godfrey!

In 1678 British magistrate Sir Edmund Berry Godfrey, who had recently presided at the trials of Roman Catholics accused of plotting against King Charles II, was found murdered. Suspects under torture named three assassins who (although probably innocent) were executed near the site of the killing, on Greenberry Hill (now Primrose Hill), London. Their names were Green, Berry and Hill.

Money for old rope

A British newspaper in the 1860s reported gamblers would pay up to £8 (then c.$50, a month's pay for a skilled worker) for a small piece of hangman's rope, a charm to guarantee success at cards.

Unlucky Merman

12th century chronicles tell how fishermen at Orford, England, caught a naked, shaggy 'wild man' in their nets. They took him to be a Merman (a man living in the sea, not the fish-tailed version), for he swam like an eel;

ate raw fish; knew nothing of Christianity; and did not speak 'even when hung up by his feet

boarding, they met a priest, lawyer or crosseyed person. Aboard, bad luck was certain if anyone mentioned rabbits or whistled, if a woman was aboard, or the ship's name ended in 'a'. Sailors took care never to lend an undamaged article or sew during a storm. They saw it as tempting fate to learn to swim, preferring to wear gold earrings as a charm against drowning.

▼ Pig girl

'Wolf children' (below) are usually said to be found or stolen by their animal foster parents – but a Chinese 'pig girl' left her human family by choice. Born on a farm near Canton, Cho-Lee preferred pigs as playmates to her brothers or twin sister, and at the age of three, despite parental protest, moved into the pigsty for good. Until she was five she lived on sow's milk; later she joined her friends at the trough. Locals who tried to 'rescue' her were driven off by the pigs. An animal behaviourist who studied the odd 'family' found Cho-Lee was of normal intelligence – and concluded she just enjoyed making a pig of herself.

a kind of fish bearing resemblance to humanity, or an evil spirit lurking in the body of a drowned man'. History does not record his eventual fate.

◄ Lucky for some

If tales of a certain Mrs. Murray are true, she may have been a 'Jonah', dooming the ships she travelled in, but her own luck was certainly amazing. This legendary lady is said to have survived the *Titanic* disaster (left); the torpedoing and sinking of the liner *Lusitania* in 1915; and the loss of the liner *Celtic*, rammed and sunk in 1927.

Wary sailors

Sailors are more superstitious than most. Until recently seamen would not sail on Fridays, and were reluctant to do so if, before

Lady Wonder: equine oracle

In the 1930s-50s crowds flocked to see Lady, or Lady Wonder, the 'talking horse' of Richmond, Va., answer questions via a kind of giant typewriter. They were not the usual maths queries offered to 'educated animals', but requests for predictions. The most unusual prophetess accurately forecast election winners and sport results, located lost property and was even consulted by the police in missing persons cases. Research scientists concluded she had real psychic power. But a striking feature in contemporary reports is the strong dislike the 'loathsome-looking mare' aroused in many who consulted her. Often she exposed forgotten scandals and tragedies, and 'clients' left in tears, accusing her owners of trafficking with the Devil.

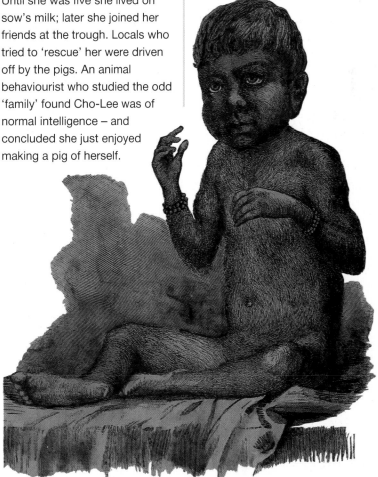

and cruelly tortured'. His captors kept him two months, but never decided if he was 'mortal man, or

INDEX

PICTURE CREDITS

The publishers wish to thank the following agencies and individuals who have supplied photographs for this book. The photographs have been credited by page number and, where necessary, by position on the page: B(Bottom), T(Top), L(Left), BR(Bottom Right), etc.